WORLD HISTORY

The Americas Before 1492

WORLD
HISTORY

WORLD HISTORY: THE AMERICAS BEFORE 1492

Copyright © 2011 by Morgan Reynolds Publishing

Library of Congress Cataloging-in-Publication Data

Cunningham, Kevin, 1966-
The Americas before 1492 / by Kevin Cunningham. -- 1st ed.
    p. cm.
Includes bibliographical references and index.
ISBN 978-1-59935-143-8
1. Civilization--America. 2. Civilization, Ancient. 3. Indians--History.
4. Indians--Antiquities. 5. America--Antiquities. I. Title.
E58.C86 2011
973'.01--dc22

                              2010017974

PRINTED IN THE UNITED STATES OF AMERICA
First Edition

Book cover and interior designed by:
Ed Morgan, navyblue design studio
Greensboro, NC

WORLD
HISTORY

THE AMERICAS BEFORE 1492

Kevin Cunningham

GREENSBORO, NORTH CAROLINA

Table of Contents

Chapter One:
A Past Evolving Over Time

The story used to be fairly simple.

According to the traditional version of history, the Western Hemisphere of 1492 consisted of two large continents inhabited by a few million human beings misnamed Indians by Christopher Columbus. The Indians, the account went on, lived for the most part in scattered bands, hunting and gathering, or fishing and gathering, with a small percentage living together in permanent farming villages. Their lifestyles, though differing from place to place, were simple and sustainable—they lived in harmony with nature, left little if any mark upon the land, and did not change it for the better any more than they had for the worse.

Evolution, or progress, in the Americas had ceased millennia before Europeans arrived. There had been no advancements in technology, religious thought, political systems, or social organization. The Arawaks, who greeted Columbus, and all of the other indigenous peoples of the Western Hemisphere lived as their ancestors had lived—never changing their ways or moving their homes, in essence having no history to speak of. Even the two cultures that history books recognized as relatively more advanced—the Inca and the Aztec—were primitive and lacked technology. Both cultures, and several others capitulated to small groups of Spanish horsemen armed with guns, proving the superiority of European culture over that of the Americas.

In the last fifty years, however, research findings have disproved virtually every idea expressed above, leading historians to reject that traditional view. Archaeologists, anthropologists, geneticists, and linguists keep finding evidence of greater and grander accomplishment—of peoples who altered their environments for food and comfort; of city complexes almost as old as those of the Middle East; and of technological innovation.

These discoveries about the Native American peoples have prompted scientists and historians not only to reevaluate the history of North and South America on both sides of the 1492 divide, but also to assess the development of pre-Columbian Native American culture in isolation from that of the world's other great civilizations. Until recently, scholars measured progress according to the trajectory of Western culture, but the more they learn, the more aware they are of how sophisticated Native American civilizations had become. Even putting aside the insights provided by modern technology, it is striking that it took thoughtful, inquiring minds half a millennium to acknowledge the influence Native American cultures had in shaping the "New World."

Before addressing its profound technologies and tracing the roots of its people, let us first get a sense of what one of the Americas' foremost empires around 1492 was like—as seen through the eyes of Spanish conquistadors led by General Hernán Cortés.

Hernán Cortés de Monroy y Pizarro (1485 – 1547) was a Spanish conquistador who led an expedition that caused the fall of the Aztec empire.

Tenochtitlan: A Great Metropolis

Located on a crystal blue volcanic lake, Tenochtitlan had gone in two centuries from an unwanted island to the seat of an organized government that dominated Mesoamerica from the Pacific Ocean to the Gulf of Mexico. It was no village, but a metropolis of stone, wood, and adobe inhabited by 200,000 to 250,000 people, making it the largest city in the Western Hemisphere and one of the three or four largest on earth.

The Spanish declared it magnificent. Bernal Díaz del Castillo, a conquistador and lieutenant of General Cortés, wrote down impressions from their arrival in 1519:

> And when we saw all those cities and villages built in the water, and other great towns on dry land, and that straight and level causeway leading to [the city], we were astounded. These great

11

A hand-colored nineteenth century woodcut reproduction of an early Spanish colonial map depicting Tenochtitlan, the capital of Aztec, Mexico

towns . . . and buildings rising from the water, all made of stone, seemed like an enchanted vision . . . . Indeed, some of our soldiers asked whether it was not all a dream. . . . It was all so wonderful that I do not know how to describe this first glimpse of things never heard of, seen, or dreamed of before.

In Tenochtitlan's city center stood a sacred district walled off from the rest of the city. Temples atop pyramids dominated the skyline, with some of the highest of these magnificent structures—one dedicated to Huitzilopochtli, the God of War, and another to the rain god Tlaloc—towering almost two-hundred feet (sixty meters) high. It is estimated that roughly eighty other religious buildings filled out the precinct.

This sacred district served as the city's hub, with the main streets radiating from it at points due north, south, east, and west—a layout modeled upon religious architecture.

Small pyramids dedicated to the minor deities of the Mexica pantheon dotted the cityscape, and statues painted in vivid colors stood around temples and in public places. Across the city, canoes by the hundred if not thousand navigated a maze of canals to bring in products and tribute, collect human waste for use as fertilizer, and deliver fresh water brought in from shore by an aqueduct system that ran parallel to one of the three causeways that connected Tenochtitlan to the shore. As for the citizens, the elite built palaces of red rock, while everyone else lived in white adobe houses. Craftspeople—goldsmiths, potters, and others—congregated in their own neighborhoods.

The Mexica had increased the size of their island by using rock and mud as landfill. In addition, they created chinampas, gardens built on artificial mud islands that were watered by the lake.

Tenochtitlan was the senior partner in the Triple Alliance, a power bloc it shared with Toccoco, a city on the lake's eastern shore, and Tacuba, a much smaller town located beyond the causeway that led west. Bustling markets featured products brought in from the fifty or so towns that paid allegiance to the Alliance: rare green quetzal feathers the nobles sought to decorate their persons; flint for weapons and obsidian for razor-sharp knives used in human sacrifice; slaves; salt; and maize, the cornerstone of the Mexica diet. Merchants and commoners alike placed such a high value on cacao, the basis of chocolate, that they used the beans as money.

Tenochtitlan had schools, "houses of youth," to teach girls housekeeping and boys how to fight. Priests practiced astronomy, interpreted the Mexica's complex calendar, and held great power through their control of sacred rituals and festivals. Judges in the Mexica's legal system heard cases while foot messengers carried commands to outlying towns. The ruler, called an emperor by Europeans and *tlatoani* (spokesman) in the local language, kept a zoo, botanical gardens, and even a display of deformed human beings.

Defying Traditional Views: More Evidence, Less Consensus?

What we know of Tenochtitlan, then, defies the traditional views that pre-Columbian Americans lacked technology and that they lived in static (unchanging) societies. History had moved for the Mexica, and if historians for a long time had trouble believing it, the Mexica did not. In well-honed speeches and in folding books painted on bark paper, the Mexica's nobles and priests and poets returned again and again to their own glorious past. If they made up large parts of that past to boost Tenochtitlan's credibility—and it appears they did—it simply made their rulers as conniving as those found in other lands the world over.

The Mexica's society, then, evolved. So did the Triple Alliance, and the peoples in the fifty cities under it, and the

ON THE CANAL.

A hand-colored nineteenth century illustration depicting Mexica merchants on a canal in Tenochtitlan before the Spanish conquest

tens of millions of human beings living up and down what came to be called the New World.

Every new piece of evidence unearthed by archaeologists faces a healthy scientific skepticism. Evidence provides a basis for theories, the framework of ideas that scientists and the rest of us use to understand aspects of the world. A theory may stand up to challenges and a sort of general agreement with it—a consensus—may take root. Or it may not. Often a new theory and the opposition to it compete for decades as researchers dig for more evidence to support their view.

Illustrated by the example of Tenochtitlan, the story of the Americas before 1492 is a story of controversies. In fact, if you read enough pre-Columbian history, it sounds like scholars can't agree on anything; that what we "know" is really a mountain of maybes. That isn't quite true. And, regardless, wherever a person may stand on a contentious issue, one thing is beyond dispute: the story isn't simple—and the past is evolving over time.

Chapter Two:
Solving Prehistory's Mysteries

In 1590 Jesuit scholar José de Acosta, a missionary with experience in Peru and Mexico, proposed an unusual origin for the indigenous peoples he had encountered during his career. Native Americans, he claimed, came from Asia. It was an unusual idea at the time, to say the least. In 1590, Europeans had only a dim idea of northeast Asia's geography. That a narrow strait separated Eurasia from North America was unknown, except perhaps to those living in the region.

Acosta's suggestion was just one of a number of theories that Europeans conceived to explain Native American origins. Those looking to biblical scripture believed that New World peoples had perhaps descended from the lost tribes of Hebrews mentioned in the Old Testament. Others of a more historical bent proposed that sea explorers from an ancient Old World civilization—Carthage, Egypt, even mythical Atlantis—found a way to the Americas and fathered the Native Americans. Christopher Columbus died believing he had landed in Asia, and that the Indians he met were of that continent.

Indigenous peoples had their own explanations. Although origin stories varied from culture to culture and even among groups within a single culture, most Native Americans generally believed that their gods had placed their ancestors in the Americas, and that they had always lived there.

Science, fortified by new methods and philosophies, upended most of the explanations—except Acosta's. The new hypothesis that emerged out of scientific inquiry was supported by the renderings of a modern map. About fifty-five miles (ninety kilometers) of water, known as the Bering Strait, separates Siberia and Alaska. During the last ice age, however, the strait's ocean floor was dry land and open to a human migration.

While this idea sounded like common sense, evidence to support it was elusive—until 1990. That year, a new type of genetic testing provided the support for the hypothesis. Strictly speaking, nothing in science is ever proven, but an Asian origin for Native Americans is one of the few things that contemporary scholars agree upon. One of the reasons for that concensus is the strong evidence presented by a technique that tests mitochondrial DNA (mtDNA), which is passed down from mothers to children of both sexes.

Genetics researcher Douglas C. Wallace, a pioneer in mtDNA testing, and molecular anthropologist Tad Schurr led a team that took mtDNA samples from living Native Americans. More than 96 percent of those sampled carried mitochonria from groups designated A, B, C, and D, with a small number from a rare group designated X. All four of the major groups were also found in Asian testees. Native Americans and certain populations in Asia had descended from common ancestors. Acosta had been right.

Beringia: The Gateway to America

The ancestral Native Americans are often said to have crossed a land bridge called Beringia that connected Siberia and the

The Bering Strait separates the United States and the Russian Federation by only fifty-six miles.

northwestern tip of North America. At its widest point, this land mass stretched about 1,000 miles (1,609 kilometers) from north to south—roughly the distance from Minneapolis to New Orleans—and also included the area between the Lena River in Siberia and the Mackenzie River in North America.

Beringia owed its existence to the ice age, or rather, to multiple ice ages within a cycle of advancing and retreating glaciers. During glacials, immense ice sheets thickened and spread out across North America. As ice sheets amassed, they locked up such huge amounts of seawater that ocean levels fell around the world. In turn, as the seas became shallower, Beringia emerged.

When the world's climate warmed during interglacials, the ocean nibbled away at the land. Parts of Beringia always remained above water, however, until the Pleistocene Era waned about 11,000 years ago. Another interglacial began, the one we live in today, and the Bering Strait has separated the continents ever since.

Contrary to common perception, the hunters didn't sprint across to the uninhabited Western Hemisphere. There was no need to hurry. During Beringia's last phase the intercontinental crossing remained above water for 16,000 years. Beringia's basically treeless and featureless terrain presented few natural obstacles to people on the move. Eventually, the hunters moved east into the modern-day Yukon. There, they did meet an impassable barrier: the Pleistocene ice sheets.

The larger of the two ice masses, the Laurentide Glacier, was a number of glaciers that had coalesced into a single sheet. A second, the Cordilleran Glacier, covered the Aleutian Islands, western Canada, and at its peak a sliver of the northwestern U.S.

About 28,000 years ago, the two ice sheets met on the Canadian plains and closed off the land further south. The area between the two partially opened during warm interglacials—one scientist compared it to the glaciers unzipping from the north and south—but the Laurentide and Cordilleran did not completely part until around 13,000 years ago.

At first the ice-free corridor was a dead region scoured by glacial ice. Winds off the remaining glaciers kept the climate cold. Vast lakes, formed from meltwater off the ice sheets, made the land mostly, if not entirely, impassable.

But plants and animals returned as the ice sheets continued to melt. At some point, Pleistocene hunters could have used the corridor to enter areas further south—today's southern Canada and continental U.S. For decades, in fact, archaeologists and others assumed that this corridor was the route used by the ancestors of Native Americans. Once through the corridor, the thinking went, people spread south.

That theory is disputed today. But another question has caught the attention of genetics research: exactly how many of these pioneers made the journey into the unknown lands south of the glaciers?

Making the Transcontinental Trek

Research about who made this journey has yielded competing theories. The small number of mtDNA groups found in modern Native Americans—the four major types and three more carried by far smaller numbers of individuals—suggests that Native Americans descended from a small population of founders. Otherwise, there would be greater genetic diversity. In 2005, for instance, a researcher at Rutgers University's Department of Genetics proposed that the founding population was only seventy to eighty people. Other scientists have suggested a few hundred to perhaps as many as 5,400 founders. The latter figure appears to be the maximum number one can project using the available mtDNA evidence.

That brings us to when Pleistocene hunters entered the rest of the Americas, one of the long-raging battles in American archaeology. To get a sense of it requires stepping aside from the usual flow of what happened first, then next, and instead examining how archaeological discoveries established our timeline for prehistory.

Signs Pointing to Clovis

At the turn of the twentieth century, the consensus among those in the still-fledgling field of archaeology was that humans had not inhabited the Western Hemisphere during the Pleistocene. That idea was overturned in the 1920s by the discovery of a stone point embedded in a bison skeleton found near Folsom, New Mexico.

Another discovery soon pushed back mankind's presence in North America even further. In 1932, gravel miners stumbled onto massive fossil bones outside of Clovis, New Mexico. Edgar B. Howard, hearing of the find, left his office at the Academy of Natural Sciences at the University of

Pennsylvania and boarded a westbound train. Recognizing the site's potential, Howard secured permission to dig and began work the next spring. Through the summer of 1933 he and his team found unusual stone points of lesser quality than those at Folsom and, by implication, evidence of an even earlier culture. Subsequent excavations uncovered more points in the bones of mammoths and other animals.

As time passed, more discoveries revealed that Paleo-Indians using the Clovis-style points and tools had killed and butchered prey at sites in all of the lower forty-eight United States and Mexico, though rarely farther south.

The Clovis point was unique to the Americas. None have turned up elsewhere, not even in Siberia, where one might expect to find a related, if earlier, technology. The typical Clovis point had telltale grooves called flutes chipped out of it on each side. The flutes ran part of the length of the point and a sharp edge ran part of the way down each side. Typically, the point's base was smooth, likely to enable a hunter to tie it to a wooden shaft. From base to tip a point measured around ten centimeters long and three wide, though this is an average, as Clovis points came in many sizes and shapes.

A four-inch-long portion of a Clovis point, circa 10,000 BC

David Kilby of the University of New Mexico clarified the usefulness and ingenuity behind these pieces, saying, "Clovis points, arguably, represent the state of the art in hunting weapons on Earth at the time and are probably capable of taking down just about any animal on the late Pleistocene landscape." Considering the size of some late-Pleistocene mammals—mammoths and a nineteen-foot-long giant sloth being but two—it sounds like a bold claim. But in fact archaeologists have unearthed Clovis points stuck in or near the bones of many large animals.

The age and ubiquity of Clovis tools convinced a majority of archaeologists that the original Paleo-Indians all belonged to the Clovis culture. In 1964, University of Arizona archaeologist C. Vance Haynes laid out what came to be known as the Clovis First model.

Haynes proposed that around 13,000 to 14,000 years ago, a series of events led to the populating of the Western Hemisphere. At that time, Haynes said, hunters crossed Beringia and rushed through the ice-free corridor just before Beringia sank. Once through the glaciers, Paleo-Indians fanned out across North America and hunted giant herbivores with their Clovis point technology. Eventually, the Paleo-Indians and their descendants moved into Central and South America. In Haynes's view, all of the peoples of the Western Hemisphere descended from an original Clovis culture.

"Clovis First" or Second?

The Clovis First idea hardened into accepted fact—the media reported it as truth, textbooks taught it as same. Many professional archaeologists accepted Haynes's assertion so completely that they quit digging after they found Clovis tools because they were sure no other artifacts could be buried farther down.

Meanwhile, archaeologists open to the idea of earlier, pre-Clovis peoples found themselves tasked not only with finding beyond-indisputable evidence, but also with convincing an archaeological mainstream that was increasingly skeptical—if not hostile—to the very idea. The ensuing feuds turned bitter, escalating to charges of incompetence and accusations that individual archaeologists planted artifacts in pre-Clovis layers of soil. On the other side, those open to the pre-Clovis idea called Clovis First proponents closed-minded and nick-named them the "Clovis police."

American archaeologist Tom Dillehay was teaching in Valdavia, Chile, when he saw artifacts unearthed at Monte Verde, a site located on a creek south of the city. In 1977, Dillehay and a team began to dig, and over the next nine years, close to eighty collaborators working in a variety of disciplines excavated Monte Verde and analyzed their finds.

What they found upended conventional views of how and when mankind entered the Americas.

Monte Verde had survived due to rare circumstances. Not long after a group of twenty or thirty prehistoric humans departed, the creek backed up. Peat matted with grass and saturated with water covered the buildings and objects that had been abandoned. The lack of oxygen in the peat slowed the process of decay, and the remains, including organic material unheard-of at American sites of such great age, were preserved.

Fruit, wood, seeds, meat, seaweed, hide, pieces of seventy-five plant species—it was a treasure trove, albeit one that required painstaking work to save. Study showed that some of the plants had been cooked; that the people had drank a boldo-leaf-and-seaweed tea still used by locals as a medicine; that they used tools of wood and stone and ivory; and that they ate plants harvested from the nearby Andes Mountains and the ocean. The discovery of huts in the vicinity yielded bones and food, lengths of knotted string, tools, clay hearths, and, most dramatically, a child's footprint preserved in sandy clay.

This organic material allowed for radiocarbon dating. Using multiple laboratories to check one set of results against another,

Timeline: The Late Pleistocene Era

28,000 years ago	Ice-free corridor closes
27,000	Beringia begins to emerge from beneath the ocean as sea levels fall
18,000	Last Glacial Maximum marks peak of Ice Age
18,000	Beringia at or near its maximum size
16,000	Pacific coastal route partially opens for 1,500-year period
14,500	Laurentide and Cordilleran Glaciers retreat
13,400	Pacific coastal route opens for good
12,500	Human presence at Monte Verde site in Chile
11,500	Ice-free corridor becomes passable
11,500–10,900	Clovis culture dominates North America
11,300	Human presence at Clovis site in New Mexico
11,000	Bering land bridge severed by rising oceans
10,960	Human presence on islands off the California coast
10,900	Clovis culture vanishes
10,000	Pleistocene ends, Holocene (modern era) begins

Dillehay discovered that some of the artifacts dated back to at least 11,790 years ago (give or take two hundred years), while others were from 13,565 years ago (give or take 250 years). Dillehay, aware the findings were explosive, announced a date of 12,500 years ago—long before Clovis—as an estimate for human settlement at Monte Verde.

The issue of the site's age turned into an epic academic battle fought with papers and field reports, news articles, and conference lectures. In 1997, archaeologists on both sides, including Haynes and Dillehay, held a sort of on-the-go debate on Monte Verde. They examined artifacts in Chile and at an archive at the University of Kentucky, where Dillehay was teaching. They also discussed the about-to-be-published 1,000-page opus in which Dillehay and his team had presented their findings. Finally, they journeyed to Monte Verde.

The debate, though thorny, ultimately yielded a consensus. The participants accepted that artifacts from Monte Verde dated to 12,500 years ago—before Clovis.

A published statement from the group carried great weight, but it hardly ended the controversy. Haynes backtracked somewhat, and other Clovis First advocates challenged what they perceived as errors in Dillehay's research. Opinion nonetheless shifted in favor of Monte Verde's age and the idea that Clovis was not first, after all.

Digging at Monte Verde and Raising New Questions

Monte Verde nevertheless raised new questions. The oldest confirmed site of human settlement in the entire Americas was farther from the ice-free corridor than any other, farther by thousands of miles, in fact almost as far as you can get from Beringia while staying on dry land. Since no one doubts an Asian origin for the Paleo-Indians, how did prehistoric hunters cover so much ground in what anthropologists consider the blink of an eye?

An excavated structure thought to be a medicine hut at the Monte Verde archaeological site in south-central Chile. The wishbone-shaped structure contains several masticated cuds that consist of seaweed and other plants.

Genetic testing and new finds may answer that question if either, or both, confirm a first wave of settlers entered the unglaciated regions of North America earlier than is now believed. If prehistoric hunters bypassed the ice sheets 15,000 years ago or 20,000 years ago, their descendants would have had more time to wander as far as Monte Verde. That proposition is far from proven, however, and it still leaves us to wonder how the hunters made the trip.

With that hypothesis in mind, some archaeologists began to investigate an alternative to the ice-free corridor. What if the Pleistocene hunters went around the glaciers by boating or walking down the Pacific coast? Support for this idea springs

Paisley Caves in Oregon:
Site of a Pre-Clovis Culture?

Intriguingly, one of the possible pre-Clovis sites under investigation lies near the proposed coastal route. Located in southern Oregon, the Paisley 5 Mile Point Caves has attracted archaeological attention since the 1930s. In 2002 and 2003, a team discovered coprolites—fossil feces—that contained enough mitochondrial DNA for testing.

The coprolites turned out to have mtDNA from both the A and B haplogroups, a result consistent with mtDNA tests on Native Americans. Radiocarbon tests, meanwhile, dated the oldest coprolite matter to before 12,000 years ago, perhaps as long as a thousand years prior to the appearance of Clovis artifacts in the archaeological record. "Our findings show that there were people south of the ice cap several hundred years before the ice-free corridor developed," said Eske Willerslev, a leading researcher in ancient DNA who conducted part of the test regimen. "The first humans either had to walk or sail along the American west coast to get around the ice cap . . . unless they arrived so long before the last ice age that the land passage wasn't yet blocked by ice."

Though dissenters suggested the coprolites came from dogs—the team did find canine DNA, as well—the find at Paisley Caves has been taken seriously. Work at the site continues.

from the notion that what was possible elsewhere could have happened in North America. Australia's first peoples, for example, traveled in simple boats from Asia at least 40,000 years ago, and they crossed a strait perhaps fifty-five miles (ninety kilometers) wide.

But skeptics point out that crossing the tropical seas north of Australia differed from floating a boat made of animal hides through the freezing water and floating ice off the coast of North America during the Ice Age. At the same time, however, scholars accept that Paleo-Indians in later generations used watercraft to reach the Channel Islands off California around 10,960 years ago. If they used boats, perhaps their ancestors did, too.

Although the ice advanced to the sea in places, it is possible that pockets of land remained open along the northern coast. The Pleistocene explorers, the theory goes, could have hopscotched from one oasis to the next, hunting and fishing along the way, and gathering berries or other food at the oases as the climate and seasons allowed.

It is also possible that the hunters walked. During periods of low sea levels, the continent's Pacific coast extended as much as fifty miles farther west, perhaps beyond the reach of the ice.

Finding evidence to support any version of a coastal theory will be a challenge. Much of the proposed land route is now underwater, as are many of the hypothetical oases used by the hypothetical sailors. Hope exists, however. Geological forces have raised sections of the ice age coastline above today's sea level. Artifacts that confirm the coastal route may await discovery beneath the coastal forests of Alaska or British Columbia.

The coastal route theory is still disputed. In a year or ten years it may be considered embarrassingly wrong. As Monte Verde showed, however, a single discovery can rewrite the history books. Archaeologists realize that another site may one day unseat Monte Verde as the hemisphere's oldest pillar of

Native American ruins at Hovenweep National Monument, in Cortez, Colorado. Human habitation at Hovenweep dates back more than 10,000 years, when nomadic Paleo-Indians visited the Canyon Mesa to gather food and hunt game. At Hovenweep, there are six clusters of prehistoric Puebloan-era villages spread over a twenty-mile expanse along the Utah-Colorado border.

civilization—in fact, several contenders already have been proposed. A find on the Canadian plains may return the ice-free corridor to its old prominence. Another in Siberia or Alaska or the Yukon could push the human passage through Beringia farther back on the timeline of history.

For now, however, the consensus is that people had spread into parts of the Americas by 12,500 years ago and had probably arrived in Beringia long before that. Their descendants filled two continents, mastered environments from the Arctic to the Amazon, and created a breathtaking variety of cultures that developed without outside influence until Columbus made his fateful landing in 1492.

Chapter Three:
Forgotten Cities

Caral is one of perhaps twenty-five towns located in the Norte Chico (Spanish for *little north*), a 165-acre archaeological site north of Lima, Peru. At Caral, pyramids with ramps and staircases set in the sides rise as high as six stories (eighteen meters). Smaller pyramidal mounds, each with its own design, surround wide-open plazas dug one-to-two yards (0.9 to 1.8 meters) into the ground.

To erect the mounds, the builders wrapped pieces of granite and other stone in mesh bags of woven grass harvested in the nearby highlands. These sacks of rock served as a foundation and reinforcement for the terraces built into the mounds. The stone and mortar walls in the mounds show signs of repair and rebuilding, as well as continual repainting. Fires burned at a temple complex, crowds gathered at an amphitheater. Prominent citizens occupied houses with painted walls located near, or connected to, the pyramids. Others lived in adobe houses, the poorest of them settling for cane and mud structures.

Despite the presence of the nearby Pacific and four rivers gushing down from the Andes, the Norte Chico is amazingly dry. Parts of it receive perhaps two inches (five centimeters) of rain per year, most of it in the form of moisture leached from the fog that rolls in on winter mornings.

Ruth Shady Solis, a Peruvian archaeologist, began work there in the 1990s on a site along the Supe River about fourteen miles (twenty-three kilometers) from the coast. She and a ragtag band of workers—including soldiers borrowed from the Peruvian army—uncovered the base of a six-story pyramid measuring five-hundred feet by four-hundred feet at its base and topped with an upper terrace of rooms, stairways, and hearths. Archaeologists consider this kind of monumental architecture one of the telltale signs of a complex human society.

In the course of digging Shady found organic material like wood and a type of grass used to make sacks. Radiocarbon dating showed some of the artifacts dated from 2600 BC. The Norte Chico was the oldest urban area in the Americas by far—in and of itself a spectacular finding. But the dates placed the Caral pyramids as far back in history as the far more famous pyramids of Egypt.

In other words, the cities of the Norte Chico are among the earliest cities to arise anywhere.

As Shady noted, the people at Caral and elsewhere in the Norte Chico had no contact with other complex societies.

"The people who built the first of these structures had no model to go by, no precedent to use in building a monument," said Winifred Creamer, an American archaeologist at the Norte Chico and part of the radiocarbon dating team. "It's a bit like deciding to build a functioning spaceship in your back yard, and succeeding."

Just as significantly, they organized a government, a necessary component for running a complex society. Building pyramids, for example, requires leaders to conceive the plans, organize workers, and keep things moving, as well as followers like artisans to work stone and laborers to haul it and build with it.

Wari and Tiwanaku: Norte Chico's Descendant Neighbors

City-building caught on along the coast and in the mountains to the east. A number of small states rose and fell after the Norte Chico's demise. About AD 600, however, a pair of powerful kingdoms appeared in the Andes Mountains.

Wari and Tiwanaku borrowed architectural and spiritual elements from earlier Andean cultures influenced by Norte Chico cities. But otherwise they were very different, despite being neighbors. Wari appeared at a time when the El Niño weather pattern had changed central Peru's climate for the worse. A severe El Niño can cause droughts capable of shattering a culture. In fact, El Niño-related climate change may have helped drive the pyramid-builders from the Norte Chico.

Studies show that rainfall in parts of the Andes declined as much as 30 percent in the late sixth century. But the Wari adapted to the drier climate by implementing irrigation techniques that steered Andean snowmelt to terraced fields at high elevations less affected by the El Niño changes. Their system opened up hundreds of thousands of acres of farmland on land so cold and steep that today three-quarters of it lies empty.

The Wari capital, also called Wari, may have had tens of thousands of inhabitants at its height. Its citizens erected a city of trapezoid and rectangular building complexes separated by high walls and narrow streets. Each complex had drains, a patio, apartments built on a grid, workspaces, and narrow halls that may have been storage areas.

As the Wari people spread out, they built similar, if smaller, copies of their capital throughout their growing empire. The towns, built on a uniform template, and with their buildings and walls glowing with white paint, concentrated on trade and influencing the indigenous cultures of a given region. Their military purpose, if any, is unknown.

At the southern end of the empire sat an odd mountain settlement today known as Cerro Baúl. Located atop a water-less mesa, Cerro Baúl overlooked territory controlled by the Tiwanaku, another expanding Andean culture. A fifteen-mile-long canal brought water to the foot of the mountain. From

Warfare and the Expansion of Empires

According to one theory, warfare played a part in the formation of all early cities and was in fact as important to the process as agriculture or pottery. But that doesn't appear to be the case in the Norte Chico. Jonathan Haas, a scholar on the subject, went there expecting to find evidence of violence in the region. He came up empty. There were no defensive walls, no bodies exhibiting signs of violent death. He and his collaborators suggest city rulers weren't warlords but religious leaders who didn't need fear or force to get followers to build the pyramids. Instead, communities undertook such projects out of religious devotion, as happened later in other New World urban complexes. Feasts, with music provided by people playing flutes made of pelican and condor bones, provided added incentive to get involved.

there, a line of servants handed up jars of water, one after the other, to supply the elite living on the mesa.

Why the Wari chose Cerro Baúl is unknown. Perhaps they sought the mountain's power as an *apu*, a spirit force made solid. Perhaps they wished to impress or influence the Tiwanaku or set up a settlement to head off Tiwanaku expansion. Control of local trade is another possibility. At least in part they probably wanted to use the mesa's height to elevate themselves closer to the gods.

What we know for sure is that the Wari built an important structure atop Cerro Baúl—a brewery.

The brew of choice was a corn beer called *chicha*. Making it was no easy process, as brewing requires a lot of water. The laborers sending buckets of it up the mountainside would have worked very long hours whenever it was time to brew a new batch. The brewery's female staff, meanwhile, used fires fueled by llama and guinea pig dung to boil the ingredients.

According to archaeologist Donna Nash of the Field Museum in Chicago, the Wari living there may have used the beer to smooth relations with the Tiwanaku. Nash believes that parties, rather than conquest, facilitated Wari influence over towns and trade.

"The Wari were an early experiment in empire-building," said Katharina Schreiber, an archaeologist at the University of California-Santa Barbara. "They had no history of prior empires, no precedent to look back on. They found it takes very different strategies to control different places."

Not that Wari society was untouched by violence. Although archaeologists have found little evidence suggesting those at Cerro Baúl engaged in war, works of art and the discovery of skulls used as display trophies suggest that as part of their rituals, the Wari beheaded prisoners captured in distant regions. Craftspeople skinned the skulls. Cords were then strung through a hole so that the trophies could be carried around.

Research indicates that the Wari abandoned Cerro Baúl around AD 1000. After a feast, two dozen lords smashed half-gallon ceramic cups called keros and burned the brewery to the ground. Wari civilization vanishes from the archaeological record shortly after that date.

At the time the Wari were building their empire, the Tiwanaku people had already lived in the Lake Titicaca region for centuries. The city of Tiwanaku, the spiritual center on the lake's southern shore, became eminent by using its religious clout to subjugate nearby towns. Akapana, a seven-level pyramid with water cascading down the sides, was a declaration of the city's power. In that way it shared a purpose with monumental architecture elsewhere in the Americas.

Tiwanaku also had aspects that were difficult to explain. The people living at Tiwanaku, for example, never finished building the city. According to anthropologist William H. Isbell and archaeologist Alexei Vranich, they never intended to. Leaders, they believe, kept areas of Tiwanaku in ruins on purpose. Ruins have an aura of authority, and ancient buildings implied that the Tiwanaku had ruled for a long time.

Whereas some parts of the city were left unfinished, other parts remained under constant construction. New building projects carried a different sort of aura, one symbolizing wealth and progress. Vranich believes Tiwanaku had few permanent inhabitants at all, that the city was a place of pilgrimage where visitors worshipped, did some sightseeing, and moved on with their faith renewed.

The Wari and Tiwanaku are only the two best-known Andean groups of the period. South of Cerro Baúl, the Nazca Indians drew giant animal and plant figures, as well as geometric symbols and miles-long straight lines, in one of the driest places on earth. The lines remained virtually unknown outside of the region until the mid-1920s, when air travel enabled archaeologists to identify the figures. The Nazca Lines have since become a world-famous tourist attraction.

Farther north, the city of Chavín de Huantar sat 10,000 feet above sea level. It faded around 200 BC.

The "Astronaut" figure at Nazca, Peru. The Nazca lines are comprised of hundreds of figures carved into the dry Peruvian desert and are estimated to be 2,000 years old, created by the Nazca people for religious or irrigation purposes.

The Moche people (AD 200–800) created storytelling murals but may have fallen victim to the El Niño droughts of the late sixth century.

The post-Wari Chimor culture battled a later series of El Niño-related setbacks with forced labor. The Chimú's capital city, Chan Chan, was built for the elite only, and they filled it with palaces and tombs and ceremonial complexes. Though sparsely inhabited by the living, Chan Chan was home to mummies, who were left sitting in their palaces and were venerated as divine beings by noble descendants.

And high up in the Andes is another mystery—the forty-mile-long Great Wall of Peru, its origins unknown, its stones mostly unexamined.

Mesoamerica: A Birthplace of Civilization

Mesoamerica, like the Andes, is considered a location of cradle civilizations, early complex societies that evolved into or influenced later cultures. Settlement there goes back to prehistory. Around 1800 BC, a society began to coalesce near Mexico's central Gulf Coast along the Coatzacoalcos River. Whereas the world's other cradle civilizations sprang up in dry or desert regions, the earliest Mesoamerican cities took root in a humid climate often soaked by rains. The flat valley was cut with flood-prone rivers that emptied into swamps. Rainfall and tropical sun fed the dynamic growth of jungle. Between the rapid spread of vegetation and the floods, the people of the region fought a constant battle to clear fields for growing their crops.

At some point the people began to tap a local tree, *Castilla elastica*, for sap. By treating the sap with heat and certain plant materials to make it supple, they turned it into rubber. This invention inspired American archaeologist George C. Vaillant to describe the people and their culture as the Olmec, a word meaning "people from the land of rubber." The term Olmec was inaccurate. In fact, Olmec isn't a word from a local language, but from Nahuatl, the language of peoples farther north. But what the Olmec called themselves will, in all likelihood, remain a mystery.

Archaeological work on the Olmec took off in 1939, when American archaeologist Matthew Stirling excavated the Tres Zapotes site in the western part of what came to be seen as the Olmec heartland. As far as Stirling could tell, the Olmec had no urbanized predecessors. The archaeological record showed scattered villages and then boom, a full-blown culture capable of monumental architecture and stunning visual art.

By 1500 BC, the Olmec had built San Lorenzo, the first of their major cities. Like several pre-Columbian population centers, however, San Lorenzo was not so much a city as we understand it but rather a ceremonial complex that glorified the nobility and the religious elite while at the same time fulfilling the religious needs of a farming population that lived in the surrounding area. The main structure was a platform 150 feet high (forty-six meters) and more than half a mile long and wide. At certain times of the year—perhaps determined by the seasons or astronomical observation—people flocked to San Lorenzo to worship and be awed by nobles and priests parading in jewels, bright feathers, and ceremonial clothing.

San Lorenzo benefited from access to a major river, the only transportation route through the thick forest. The population provided a labor force that encouraged Olmec leaders to organize public projects like the ceremonial structures, but also channels to carry away floodwater and possibly an irrigation system for crops.

No Olmec skeletons have ever been found, so archaeologists aren't sure what the people looked like. According to the artwork that has survived, the elite strapped flat pieces of wood to the foreheads of their infant children. The wood shaped the skull bones and formed long, high heads. Archaeologists have recovered thirty-seven wooden busts reflecting this look from El Manatí, a sacred burial site located in a bog southeast of San Lorenzo. Figurines found elsewhere indicate elite Olmecs also cut grooves in their teeth and pierced the septum dividing their nostrils in order to wear jewelry through the nose.

La Venta: Olmec City of Arts

San Lorenzo declined for unknown reasons after 1000 BC. But the Olmec had already started a greater city at La Venta, located to the northeast, near the eastern edge of the Olmec homeland. La Venta was built forty feet (thirteen meters) above the surrounding swamp on a rectangular island overlooking the Tonalá River. In the center was the largest and oddest New World pyramid of its age. Built of clay, it stood just over one hundred feet (thirty-one meters) high, but unlike any mound discovered elsewhere, the La Venta pyramid had a

A giant Olmec head in La Venta Park in Villahermosa, Mexico

roughly circular shape variously described as a pedaled flower or a head of garlic. (An upside-down coffee filter with a flat top is another possibility.) Columns made of basalt, a volcanic rock mined in mountains fifty miles away, provided a palisade around a plaza.

La Venta's artisans created some of the ancient world's most stunning art. Foremost among their works were four sculptures that have since become the best-known symbols of Olmec culture. The basalt sculptures, called colossal heads by archaeologists, were truly massive. Those at La Venta weighed between eleven and twenty-four tons and stood more than six feet tall. Thought to be statues of rulers, the heads were placed about the city's central plaza where their haughty expressions may have reminded passersby about who was in charge. Stylistically, the La Venta colossal heads match ten older examples found at San Lorenzo. There is one other similarity, as well: after each city fell, those who came after damaged—and then buried—the heads.

The Olmec worked rock and semi-precious stones, including imported obsidian, amethyst, amber, serpentine, clay, magnetite, and in their larger sculpted works basalt. But they considered jade the most precious stone, as did later Mesoamerican cultures. Olmec traders sought it far and wide. Scientific tests have shown the Olmec imported jade from as far away as Guatemala. Since major excavations on Olmec sites began in the 1940s, archaeologists have found jade masks, figurines that combined human and animal forms, beads, celts (axe-heads), inlays for teeth, and other worked items.

The term jade refers to a number of minerals, but the type found in Mesoamerica, jadeite, is both hard and rare. Working it into shapes was an amazing technological accomplishment for a people that lacked metal tools. "With apparent disregard for the difficulties involved," wrote archaeologist Matthew Stirling in 1961, "the tough material was managed as though it were a plastic. . . . Olmec jades rival the finest Chinese pieces, and the polish and surface texture has not been excelled by modern lapidaries."

The Olmec seemed to have spread their artistic and spiritual ideas at least in part via trade and migration. (The role of war, a common means of exporting culture elsewhere, is unclear.) Olmec pottery was sold far and wide, according to archaeological finds, and archaeologists generally believe the Olmecs traded finished goods for the raw materials found in distant regions.

It is also possible that Olmecs in many fields—pot-makers and stone-carvers, priests and architects—followed trade routes and sold their skills to nearby peoples. Note, however, this trade differed from our system of capitalists and entrepreneurs. The nobility kept total control over it, a feature of economic life the Olmec shared with Andean groups.

Practices also changed over time. San Lorenzo traded with the Oaxaca Valley to the south. But as Oaxaca grew in strength, later Olmecs, like those at La Venta, developed relationships with weaker peoples in Guatemala and elsewhere, possibly to keep the upper hand.

The Olmec deserted La Venta around 400 BC. On their way out they may have destroyed the city with their own hands. La Venta's abandonment signaled the end of Olmec dominance. Why the culture declined remains unknown. Various theories—revolt, invasion, natural disaster, disease, agricultural failures—have limited supporting evidence. The Olmec may have broken up into smaller groups on their own. Perhaps the farmers tired of the priests or the demand for labor and withdrew their support, happy to swap the high-maintenance city-complexes for a simpler way of life.

An explosion of cultural activity took place in Mesoamerica during the Olmec period. Oaxaca, located south of the Olmec heartland, was home to Monte Albán, a city and ceremonial center located 6,400 feet (1,950 meters) above sea level and visible for miles around. By 300 BC Monte Albán dominated the Oaxaca Valley. It became home to thousands of Zapotecs, until going into decline around AD 500.

Chalcatzingo, located at the base of two hills, benefited from a nearby source of fresh water, fertile soil, and white kaolin clay favored by Olmec pottery makers. After 900 BC its people adopted Olmec artistic styles, probably prospered through trade in semi-precious stones, and faded about the time the Olmec deserted La Venta. And north of the Olmec heartland, the Tlatilco culture (1200–800 BC) carved figures influenced by the Olmecs and traded obsidian with them.

North America Comes to Life

After the Olmec, Mesoamerica settled into a period of division into small political entities. Then, around 200 BC, the mysterious city of Teotihuacan rose from obscure roots in the Valley of Mexico to the north. By AD 500, it covered eight square miles and was home to between 100,000 and 250,000 people. Very few cities of its time—in either hemisphere—could match its area or population.

Teotihuacan's most commanding structure, the Pyramid of the Sun, stood two-hundred feet (sixty-one meters) high over an underground cave that may have had religious meaning. Color defined the city. Murals portrayed butterflies and human figures as well as the jaguar and serpent central to the Mesoamerican belief system. The Teotihuacano even painted the streets.

Teotihuacan fell around AD 750, perhaps to invasion by a people called the Toltecs. By then, however, towns had appeared in what would become the continental United States.

The most spectacular settlements to survive until the present day were those of the Chaco Canyon culture in southwestern North America (in present-day New Mexico). Archaeologists credit the Chaco Canyon towns, road system, and ceremonial centers to the Anasazi. The Anasazi, like the Olmec, are

The Pyramid of the Sun at Teotihuacan, outside of Mexico City

misnamed—the Navajo who moved to the area after their decline labeled them with a term meaning "ancient enemy." A modern version of the Anasazi's modular structures, with their apartment building-style rooms packed around circular ceremonial kiva, could find a place in progressive architecture today, centuries after Spanish explorers named the communal buildings pueblos.

Cities of eastern North America benefited from a climate and soil amenable to agriculture. This agrarian environment, coupled with distinctive cultural and architectural traditions, fostered the creation of urban landscapes different from those of the Southwest. Like peoples farther south, however, the so-called Eastern Woodland peoples east of the Great Plains did build earthen mounds—everywhere.

By the time Teotihuacan fell, Eastern Woodland peoples had been raising mounds for more than 4,000 years. The earliest known complex, in northern Louisiana, dates to about 3400 BC, making it older than the monuments in the more urbanized Norte Chico.

Archaeologists have found evidence of thousands of mounds in the eastern U.S., lower Canada, and the Great Plains. Around 800 BC, for example, the Adena Culture was constructing mounds over tombs laden with textiles, beads, bracelets, and large stone tobacco pipes. The Adena had a fully formed agriculture to rely upon, and during the next seven centuries their ideas spread from Indiana to maritime Canada. Some of the cultures that followed—the Hopewell and Fort Ancient, among others—continued the mound-building tradition. In the case of the Hopewell, they also spread ideas and technology, including the bow and arrow, from Chesapeake Bay north to Canada and west to Wyoming.

But mound-building found its most spectacular expression at Cahokia, the largest pre-Columbian city north of Mesoamerica.

Cahokia: Land of Maize and Mounds

Around AD 600, descendants of Hopewell peoples began to farm in the fertile river valleys near present-day St. Louis. The mishmash of tribal groups living there, all members of an umbrella culture referred to as the Mississippian, were part of an agricultural revolution. Maize, the staple crop of Mesoamerica, had in the previous centuries made its way north from the subtropics as Native American plant breeders developed a variety able to resist frost and reach maturity during shorter growing seasons.

Hopewell cultures had mostly grown maize for religious ceremonies; but the people of the river valleys discovered that the crop prospered in the rich soil. Maize became a staple food, and a population increase followed this agricultural breakthrough.

And then something remarkable happened.

University of Illinois archaeologist Timothy R. Pauketat refers to it as the Big Bang. The farmers suddenly chose to build mound complexes. Using clay to bear the weight of the earthen mound, they built the flat-topped Monks Mound, the architectural centerpiece reaching one hundred feet (thirty meters) high and covering fourteen acres. In its day Monks Mound was one of the largest structures in the Western Hemisphere. At the same time, the builders began construction on smaller mounds, avenues, a forty-acre central plaza, and playing fields for a popular game called chunkey.

Chunkey: America's First Pastime

Sports and recreational games played an important role in community life—as well as social and political organization—in ancient North America. The game of chunkey involves two teams that compete against each other by throwing spears and sticks at a rolling stone disc about the size of a hockey puck. Chunkey matches drew large crowds, and much like today, there were rivalries among supporters of competing teams. Big games were started ceremoniously by a Cahokian chief, who, standing atop the summit of one of the earthen mounds, would commence play by raising his arms. Furthermore, some archaeologists, including Pauketat, suggest that Cahokian emissaries would venture to distant lands carrying chunkey discs and spears; by introducing their sport, they formed alliances with other peoples.

Pauketat believes a local dictator may have seized power and ordered the building spree following a sign from the heavens. In 1054, a new star appeared in the constellation Taurus. Chronicles and art from Eurasian and Native American sources record that for more than three weeks it was bright enough to be visible in daytime, and that it lingered in the night sky for the better part of two years. We know today it wasn't a star but the supernova that birthed the Crab Nebula. If Pauketat is correct, the people at Cahokia—or at least the elite there—interpreted the appearance of the brilliant new "star" as a divine command to build monuments for the worship of the gods.

As is often the case in archaeology, however, there is an alternate theory. William Woods of the University of Kansas argues that those at Cahokia built the mounds as an expression of religious fervor and community pride. "Someone who was already important had a vision in the right place at the right time," he said. "People started coming in to see it and didn't want to leave the city. It was like a messianic cult, a cult of opportunity: 'Wonderful things can happen, and we all have to contribute.'"

Whatever the motives, Cahokia was an immense undertaking. The Mississippian culture, like all those in the Western Hemisphere, lacked iron tools, beasts of burden like horses and oxen, and the wheel. Without wheels for carts, and having no domesticated animals to help carry the load, the tattooed and painted Cahokians hauled dirt, clay, and timber with their own muscle power.

A Bustling Capital: Life in Cahokia

Scholars once believed that Mesoamerican culture inspired Cahokia's founders—if not directly, then through ideas carried along the trade routes. Yet archaeologists have yet to find a single artifact linking Cahokia to the cities farther south. Given the evidence uncovered until now, it appears Cahokia's

The one hundred-foot Monks Mound at Cahokia Mounds State Historic Site in Collinsville, Illinois. Monks Mound is the largest man-made earthen mound on the North American continent to date.

people, like those in the Norte Chico and the Olmec heartland, came up with the idea of a city on their own.

At its peak, Cahokia's population of 20,000 equaled that of London in the same period. It would not be surpassed by a city north of the Rio Grande until Philadelphia around 1750. Indeed, the city itself was part of a larger metropolitan area. There were 120 mounds within five miles (eight kilometers) of Cahokia and dozens more in outlying areas, plus an unknown number of villages and farms.

Still, the society buzzed around the Cahokia city center. Traders bearing products from as far away as Michigan and the Gulf of Mexico clogged the city's waterways. The workers who maintained the mounds or irrigation trenches lived nearby in log houses with steep thatched roofs; and priest-astronomers made observations using circles of wooden poles archaeologists call woodhenges. Also noteworthy was the fact that Cahokia, unlike modern cities, did not have a separate urban and rural life. Maize farmers packed onto city land right to the edge of the central plaza.

Astronomy and City Planning

In many places, buildings went up along astronomical lines, perhaps to aid in measurements, perhaps to harness spiritual energy. The Newark Earthworks, a large Hopewell site built between 100 BC and AD 500, includes an octagon linked to a circle. Every 18.6 years, the moon rises at its northernmost point—and as it climbs from the horizon its sphere splits the octagon and circle. Whole cities—from Cahokia to Tenochtitlan to Chichén Itzá—were planned at least in part to conform to astronomical phenomena like solstices and equinoxes, and the orientation of mounds, main avenues, and temple complexes usually if not always had such significance.

Most people farmed. Far fewer worked as artisans. The elite focused on decision-making and religious ritual. And Cahokian religion shared at least one aspect of its rituals with several Mesoamerican cultures: its priests and nobles practiced human sacrifice.

Cahokian priests performed the sacrificial rites with theatrical élan before large crowds. In one instance, fifty-three young women were buried simultaneously in pits, at least some clubbed to death, others still alive when they fell. Possibly the women were slaves or peasants from a village outside Cahokia—perhaps as tribute paid by subject ethnic groups. Or they may have willingly chosen to fulfill what was regarded as a vital ceremonial role.

"The women never show injury," Pauketat said. "There is no trauma. So that means either they drank poison or they were strangled. But, that's speculation. They were very carefully placed into these pits."

Two male skeletons found nearby bore signs of belonging to the nobility, which could mean that the women may have been killed to serve them. The same mound yielded more than 260 bodies killed or at least buried there at other times and perhaps for other reasons.

Evidence suggests enormous parties accompanied the human sacrifice rituals. In the 1960s, excavators discovered one of modern archaeology's holy grails—a garbage pit. This debris pile was buried so deep that the garbage had not rotted away. The excavating team fought through the breathtaking odor of 900-year-old trash and discovered 3,900 deer carcasses and almost 8,000 pots containing huge amounts of nuts, berries, maize, other foodstuffs, and tobacco seeds. Having studied the debris at length, Pauketat believes Cahokia's rulers may have held citywide celebrations complete with feasts, parades, and human sacrifice to observe special occasions or honor their rulers.

An archeological dig at Monks Mound at Cahokia Mounds State Historic Site

Overcoming Obstacles

Cahokia faltered in the 1200s. The reasons, as is often the case with pre-Columbian cultures, remain open to argument and interpretation. But it seems part of the problem was the fact the city suffered the consequences of damaging its environment. Cahokians, having stripped the land of trees, had to travel farther and farther to find wood, while the treeless land became eroded.

Woods, the University of Kansas archaeologist, believes Cahokia also had a problem with water. The city population had outgrown its water supply. The rulers addressed the problem by widening a nearby creek, but the plan backfired as disastrous floods regularly destroyed the maize fields.

The floods and other misfortunes may have undermined faith in Cahokia's rulers. The gods, it seemed, no longer favored the city. Facing a political crisis, the priestly elite did what politicians have done for thousands of years: they tried to distract people from the problem rather than solving it.

Public works increased again. Twenty thousand trees went into an expensive palisade surrounding the city's core. No one knows why the elite bothered—from all indications, Cahokia faced nothing in the way of enemy attack. To further awe the citizens, or perhaps boost their own confidence, the rulers wore more jewelry and built bigger houses.

The city then suffered another blow when an earthquake struck in the thirteenth century. An unknown portion of the city was destroyed in the quake or subsequent fires, and part of Monks Mound collapsed. The rulers tried to rebuild, but their efforts were in vain. By then people were already leaving Cahokia to capitalize on agriculture outside the city's shrinking sphere of influence. Archaeological work shows nearby mound complexes burned before being abandoned, and Woods believes Cahokia imploded in a spasm of violence and civil war. In 1350, the city was inhabited by only a handful of people.

The Mississippian culture endured nevertheless. People in the southeastern U.S. were living in villages with earthen mounds when conquistadors marauded through the region in the 1500s. But none of these towns ever approached the population and influence of Cahokia.

Chapter Four:
Harvest

The peoples of the Americas had a genius for working with plants. Their domesticated crops alone have changed the world. Imagine Italian food without tomatoes, Thai takeout without peanuts, a hamburger without French fries. For that matter, imagine a school cafeteria without peanut butter, a snack cart without chocolate or vanilla or sunflower seeds, the breakfast table without corn flakes.

The spread of Western Hemisphere plants into the rest of the world was part of what historian Alfred Crosby called the Columbian Exchange. As Crosby illustrated in his book of the same name, the Columbian Exchange was an exchange of plants, animals, human populations, ideas, and diseases between the Western Hemisphere and the Old World. The "catastrophic and bountiful effects" that followed produced repercussions in virtually every society in almost every corner of the planet.

The exchange worked both ways: New World food plants had an impact on Old World peoples and their descendants, and a handful of significant imports traveled in the opposite direction: coffee (from Ethiopia), pigs (from Europe in general), slaves (from West Africa), Christianity (first from Spain and Portugal and then from Europe in general), and smallpox (found across Eurasia in 1492).

The development of an extensive plant-based culture may have come about because Native Americans had few domesticated animals. A mass die-off of animal species during and after the Pleistocene Era had driven the New World species of horse, camel, and elephant to extinction. Native Americans, left with limited options, settled for a handful of mostly small species. In North America and Mesoamerica farmers raised turkeys, ducks, a species of honeybee, and dogs. Andean peoples added the llama and its cousin the alpaca, the guinea pig, and the semi-domesticated rhea, a large flightless bird.

Old World peoples, by comparison, kept a menagerie—the horse, camel, pig, goat, sheep, donkey, yak, reindeer, cow, honey bee, chicken, goose, duck, cat, dog, and the elephant.

For many Native American groups, hunting, fishing, and whaling fulfilled the need for meat and useful animal products like leather and bone. Even those working as part- or full-time farmers often supplemented their diet with wild game. But with the exception of people living in the vegetation-thin far north, people everywhere depended in part—and in the case of the complex societies in large part—on thousands of plants, both wild and domesticated. Of the latter, no plant transformed societies like maize.

Maize Revolution

Maize's nearest relative is teosinte, a grass native to Mexico. Teosinte stems bear between a half-dozen and a dozen hard seeds. While some scientists think Mesoamericans domesticated maize from an unknown and now-extinct ancestor, genetic evidence points to ancient farmers breeding select teosinte plants—with their small, unpromising seeds—into maize.

Five thousand cultivars, or varieties, of maize are found in Mesoamerica alone. Farmers grew it in a variety of colors— blue and black, red and gold, white and purple. Certain kinds popped when heated. The Inca in South America bred a variety as a source of sweetener, and another with huge kernels they dropped into stews.

Calculating When to Plant

Native American astronomers monitored the sky to track the seasons. At Cahokia, for example, two poles in a circle of wooden posts called a woodhenge lined up to indicate due east, the point where the sun rises on the spring and autumn equinoxes. By using the woodhenge calendar, Cahokian priests knew the dates for planting and harvesting of crops, as well as other important events.

The windows on a kiva in Chaco Canyon lined up with the point where the sun rose on the summer solstice. For a few days around the solstice, sunlight at dawn struck a niche on the wall opposite a window on the northeastern side. A ruined building at Fajada Butte seems to have served a similar purpose. At the summer solstice, a thin line of sunlight divided a man-made spiral design on the butte's wall. Six months later, the dawn of the winter solstice projected two lines of sunlight into the room. Each line struck one side of the spiral, bookending it between them.

The Seneca watched the Pleiades, a star cluster familiar to any winter stargazer in the Northern Hemisphere. When it fell below the horizon in the spring the danger of frost had passed, signaling an all-clear to plant maize. By the time the Pleiades reappeared in the fall, the fields had been harvested ahead of the first freeze.

Geneticist Nina V. Fedoroff of Pennsylvania State University called it "arguably man's first, and perhaps his greatest, feat of genetic engineering." As she told author Charles Mann, "To get corn out of teosinte . . . you couldn't get a [financial] grant to do that now, because it would sound so crazy."

Maize's successful domestication prompted ancient Mesoamericans to move from hunting and gathering into a lifestyle built around agriculture and settlement. Growth then followed a path seen in many other parts of the world. Successful agriculture created surplus food. The surplus maize could be stored for an emergency like a drought or a bad harvest, providing people with a more stable food supply. Stable food supplies led to a spike in population, and as societies got larger, there were more people to fill the labor demand for building cities.

As Mesoamerica scholar Michael D. Coe wrote, "Where [maize] flourished, so also did high culture; where it produced but scanty yields (as in many parts of western and northern Mexico), native civilization was non-existent. Maya, Aztec, Toltec, or Olmec—all depended on this staff of life."

The Maya: Maize and Milpas

The emergence of the maize-growing Maya is only partly known, and that part is complicated. But the first distinctly Mayan villages appear in the archaeological record as early as 1800 BC. Historians refer to the Mayan heyday as the Classic Period and date it from AD 200 to its sudden and still-mysterious dissolution around AD 900. During the Maya peak, a number of city-kingdoms jostled for power and influence in what today is southern Mexico, Belize, Guatemala, and Honduras.

The Maya carved their kingdoms out of tropical wilderness. Their magnificent stone pyramids, ball courts, palaces, and other structures went up in cities ruled by ahaws, or lords. Mayan cities, like those elsewhere, relied on farmers for sustenance and to provide labor. Maize production became increasingly important as the population grew and ahaws greedy for prestige and the favor of the gods made greater demands.

Mayan farmers considered maize one of the Three Sisters—along with beans and squash—at the core of their well-being. Taken together, the Sisters provided balanced nutrition. Beans, domesticated about the same time as maize, offset the protein deficiency that can come from a maize-heavy diet. Squash, meanwhile, had vitamins and like maize could be stored for use in winter or thin times. The seeds of some varieties, like pumpkin, provided protein, as well. The Three Sisters system was so successful that it spread to North America as people there took up farming the maize varieties bred for more temperate climates.

Maize's Nutritional Value

For all its benefits, maize fails to provide niacin, an essential nutrient, because the niacin in the kernels exists in a form the body cannot absorb. As a result, niacin deficiency can lead to pellagra, a debilitating and ultimately fatal disease.

Native American technology addressed the niacin problem by processing the raw corn into a more nutritious form. By 1200 BC, for example, Olmecs and other Mesoamericans had learned to boil dried maize in lime water or ashes. The process transformed the niacin in maize into a form the human body could absorb. Some archaeologists believe the boost to human health encouraged cultural development in both Mesoamerica and, later, among the mound-builders in the U.S.

The Maya grew their crops in a system, the milpa, they may have adopted from the Olmec.

A milpa derived from an age-old technique known as slash-and-burn agriculture. Farmers began by clearing trees on a patch of land. Then they burned off the remaining brush to expose the field and add the nutrient-rich ash to the soil. Fires had to burn at proper temperatures and in accordance with seasonal rains. Therefore farmers often waited days or weeks for a wind that would burn the field in the proper way. Priests in some places may have also used astronomical readings to time the sewing of a new crop. In fact, clearing the land and planting had religious significance as well as a practical application.

Next the farmer built small dirt mounds around the field. Using a planting stick, the farmer made a hole in the mound. Either he or another person then scooped a half-dozen or so seeds from a shoulder sack, dropped them in the hole, and covered them up. Hand planting allowed a farmer to choose which kinds to sew.

A milpa differed from the farms found in Europe. There were no straight rows, for one thing, and multiple crops grew together, even through and around one another.

The Three Sisters method offered many advantages. High corn shielded the beans from harsh sun while the beans used the corn stalks as bean poles. Sprawling squash plants with their large leaves protected the soil against erosion by blocking battering rains. The thick plant cover they provided also robbed weeds of sunlight. Beans, like all legumes, were exceptional at fixing important nitrogen in the soil, and in that way helped extend the amount of time a farmer could farm an area before he had to move on and create a new milpa.

Though the southern city-states were abandoned in the ninth and tenth centuries, Mayan urban culture shifted north to cities like Chichén Itzá and Uxmal. The milpa endured—the Mayan peoples of the region still use the system today—and so did maize. An account by an early European explorer left no doubt as to its central role in the Mayan diet:

> As to the meals which they ate in the time of their antiquity, they eat the same today. This is corn boiled in water and crushed. When made into dough, they dissolve it in water for a drink (pozole), and this is what they ordinarily drink and eat. An hour before sunset it was their custom to make certain tortillas of said dough. On these they supped, dipping them into certain dishes of crushed peppers, diluted with a little water and salt. Alternately with this they ate certain boiled beans of the land, which are black. They call them buul. . . . This was the only time they ate during the day, for at other times they drank the dissolved dough mentioned above.

Corn, squash, and bean plants. Indigenous peoples throughout the territory called Mesoamerica (the region of central-southeastern Mexico and northern Central America) farm using a crop growing system known as milpa. Milpa is a Mexican Spanish term that means "field" and is derived from the Nahuatl (language of the Aztecs) phrase mil-pa, meaning "to the field." Milpa agriculture produces not only corn, beans, and squash, but other crops suitable to local conditions.

Maize Fosters Ingenuity

As maize farming spread out of Mesoamerica, people everywhere invented ways to use it. Andean groups, for example, made it into *chichi*, a general term for many kinds of maize-based beverages. Mexica rulers ate a twice-baked cornbread while several North American peoples fried corn flour in animal fat to make pone. Iroquois peoples in New England and Lower Canada mixed it with maple sugar, the Zuni of the Southwest with licorice root. The Narragansett taught English colonists to make a sustaining corn-lima bean dish called succotash.

An Alternative to Maize

California had a diverse population packed into a relatively small region. Native peoples there spoke more than a hundred languages and dialects and belonged to a wide range of cultures. One food, however, appealed to people across regional and tribal lines: the acorn.

Though acorns came in many varieties, most had a bitter taste. Soaking the nuts, however, leeched out the tannins responsible. From there, women ground the acorns into a bland flour that complemented mixing with meat, shellfish, fruit, fat, insects, and other nuts. Acorn flour thickened stews and could be made into bread. Cooks added flavors to acorn mush and baked it into bread on a stove of heated rocks. Sometimes groups celebrating festivals ate mush out of communal pot with their hands. Relatedly, some cooked acorn into a semi-solid food reminiscent of gelatin or tofu.

On the other side of the Rocky Mountains, the Apache mixed acorn flour with berries and fat to make pemmican, a travel food. Native Americans in New England and California also buried caches of whole acorns for use during hard times. Acorns interred this way might remain edible for decades.

Other maize-based fare had practical benefits and, possibly, far-reaching effects. The Wari, as noted, turned corn into a sacred beer that may have helped them win friends in vulnerable areas. It is also possible that the invention of the tortilla, a durable food good for long-distance journeys, allowed Olmec traders and soldiers to spread their ideas.

Spirituality and Medicine

Native American healers combined prayer and ritual with thousands of wild, semi-domesticated, and domesticated species of plants to treat human ailments. Many of the treatments we know of were encountered after European contact. But probably some, if not most, dated back to centuries before Columbus.

Andean peoples brewed a tea from cinchona tree bark as a remedy for fevers and chills. Cinchona became the only effective treatment for malaria for three hundred years, first as "fever bark" and then as quinine, a powder made from the active ingredient in the bark.

Native Americans in eastern North America used the shrub *Hamamelis virginiana*, known to us as witch hazel, to relieve discomfort related to skin ailments, insect bites, poison ivy, and muscle pain. It remains an ingredient in several skin products and hemorrhoid medicines.

Ipecac, taken from the roots of the ipecacuanha by Brazil's Tupi-speaking peoples, brought on vomiting, and is still in use as an emetic for treating accidental poisoning. In the past it was also a treatment for deadly amoebic dysentary.

The Iroquois used cranberry roots and bark as an emetic, blood purifier, heart medicine, and as a fever treatment for infants. Medicines derived from red maple bark treated Ojibwa and Cherokee with sore eyes and Seminole athletes with back pain.

The importance of corn in today's society cannot be overestimated. Early American civilizations are credited for cultivating this important crop.

Maize inspired religious adoration. In fact, the root word, *mahiz*, meant "bread of life" to the Arawaks that Columbus met on the island of Hispaniola. The Pueblo were only one of the many cultures to offer maize to the gods. On the Great Plains, Hidasta women believed to have special powers sang to the corn to make it grow. The Maya believed the gods had carved human beings from maize, and maize stalks and tassels decorated Olmec stalae and Mesoamerican pottery.

The Inca took veneration even further. In Cuzco, the Incan capital, metal-smiths crafted a garden that made clear maize's honored place in Andean society:

> gold and silver, with their leaves, flowers and fruit; some just beginning to sprout, others half-grown, others having reached maturity. They made fields of maize with their leaves, heads, canes, roots and flowers, all exactly imitated. The beard of the maize-head was of gold, and all the rest silver, the parts being soldered together. They did the same with other plants, making the flower, or any part that became yellow, of gold, and the rest of silver.

The Potato

Although the Inca turned maize into art, the common people of the Andes depended on the potato. The potato was a generally unattractive tuber that grew in about 170 species. While the Navajo and scattered Mesoamerican peoples ate wild potatoes, active cultivation was rare in North America and may not have taken place until a short time before 1492.

The domesticated potato, as opposed to the wild kind, originated in parts of southern Peru, northeast Bolivia, and perhaps northern Chile. In its ancient pre-domesticated form it was poisonous, a reminder that it shares a plant family with the aptly-named deadly nightshade. Why Andean farmers ever chose such a toxic and bitter-tasting tuber as a potential crop is a mystery. Through the use of selective breeding, however, they had created 3,000 varieties by the time the Incas pulled together their empire in the fifteenth century.

Potatoes came in black, white, red, blue, purple, gold—practically every color a plant can hold. Some varieties were striped, others spotted, still others with a color (or colors) splashed against a plain background. Shapes varied just as much, as did flavors and suitability for long storage. Those too bitter for the human palette provided feed for llamas.

Starchy, filling, and a good source of vitamin C, the potato produced more food per acre than any other crop. Potatoes also required far less work than maize, and many varieties grew in about 60 percent of the time. Undaunted by its plainness, Andeans worked the potato into an enormous cuisine of breads, gruels, and stews.

Potatoes, like most staple foods, kept for a long time. That was especially true when people turned it into chuño.

Chuño is a type of freeze-dried potato. Different kinds were made via different processes. Typically, people in the mountains began by putting out potatoes in the nighttime's below-freezing temperatures. At daybreak they either covered the potatoes against the damaging sunlight or stomped the potatoes to squeeze out moisture. Then they repeated the process for perhaps four days and nights. The chunky white dry product that was left over then went into storage.

In Inca times, stored chuño remained edible for five or ten years. No doubt the same had been true for centuries. Archaeologists have found chuño dating from 200 BC at Tiwanaku. For any organic substance to survive that long—even in inedible form—attests to its value as an emergency food.

The Tiwanaku culture, in fact, ran on potatoes. Able to grow the tuber in great amounts, the Tiwanaku exported durable chuño, just as earlier Andean peoples had sent llama caravans loaded with chuño to the desert coastlands in exchange for cotton, fish, and other products.

If Not Maize or Potatoes, Then What?

Potatoes, though hearty, were not suited for the rain forest climate to the east of the mountains. There, people depended on the starchy root of manioc, or cassava. People in central Brazil domesticated the cassava root thousands of years ago. A good source of phosphorus, calcium, and Vitamin C, cassava root could be used in many of the same ways Andeans cooked potatoes—fried, boiled, as flour, and so on.

Cassava had great value as a staple food. Like maize and potato, it could be stored. Unlike maize, it thrived in poor soil and with minimal rainfall. The plant found a place in fields on Caribbean islands and in the Andes and Mesoamerica. After European contact, the Columbian Exchange helped transform cassava into one of the tropical world's most important foods. It is a vital part of the diet in parts of India and sub-Saharan Africa. Americans know it best as the basis of tapioca pudding.

Farmers in warmer regions cultivated the sweet potato, another nutritious root that, whatever its name, is not closely related to the potato. Arawaks on several Caribbean islands developed an agricultural system that grew sweet potatoes, pineapples, and other crops without the use of seeds. Arawak farmers instead started new plants using roots and cuttings from established plants.

The sweet potato is at the center of an archaeological mystery. Between about AD 300 and 900, it became the primary food for Polynesians, the far-ranging island peoples of the South Pacific. Yet all the criteria scientists use to trace plant origins point to the sweet potato coming from South America. For one thing, a number of varieties grow there, and species diversity is a telltale sign. In addition, some kinds grow wild. Archaeological evidence also makes clear that Andean peoples

Cassava, or manioc root. Cassava is the third-largest source of carbohydrates for people around the world.

grew sweet potatoes 5,000 years ago, long before the evidence of the plant appears in Polynesia.

Scholars and laypeople alike have advanced ideas on how the exchange took place. According to one hypothesis, sweet potato plants drifted west to Polynesia. Another proposes that Polynesian sailors island-hopped to the South American coast, found the sweet potato, and took it with them. But no theory has sufficient evidence to support it.

A variety of grains also found a place in Native American diets. Strains of amaranth, for instance, originated in Mexico thousands of years ago. The Inca called it kiwicha and considered it essential. The Mexica baked protein-rich amaranth grain into special cakes shaped like their gods. Though only grown in scattered areas of Mexico and the Andes today, amaranth has become an important cereal in South Asia and China.

Native farmers contributed a number of crops to the Eastern Agricultural Complex (EAC), a term used to describe the collective agriculture of the Eastern Woodlands people inhabiting eastern North America.

The most famous of the EAC foods was the sunflower, raised then and now for its tasty seeds and oil. Goosefoot, a relative of spinach, provided a leafy vegetable and possibly seeds. A South American species of goosefoot called quinoa was and is important in the Andes, and has become a favorite of health food enthusiasts in the U.S. Native Americans also ground seeds from maygrass and a little barley to make flour.

Cocoa: Yielding Chocolate and Riches

Of all the plant foods of the Western Hemisphere, it is doubtful any have brought more pleasure than chocolate.

Europeans and Mesoamericans had a part in giving the cacao tree the scientific name *Theobroma cacao*. In Latin *Theobroma* means "food of the gods;" cacao is a corruption of the Mayan *kakaw* (or ka'kau) and the Nahuatl word *cacahuatl*.

The cacao tree sprouts pods filled with a sweet fruit that contains fatty seeds usually referred to as beans. Processed beans are the basis of modern-day chocolate as well as the cacao drinks enjoyed in pre-Columbian America.

Scientific testing suggests the cacao plant originated in regions near South America's Amazon and Orinoco Rivers. Carried by human beings, it reached Mesoamerica in ancient times. Possibly the Olmec knew of it. Certainly the Maya did. Chocolate had a place in Mayan birth, death, and marriage rituals. A Mayan festival held in the spring honored a cacao god.

Among the Maya, *kakaw* was a popular beverage among nobles and farmers alike. Even the gods drank it, according to images on pottery. And it was a beverage only—the Maya had no chocolate bars.

Mesoamericans prepared cacao beans by mashing them into paste. After adding water, they whipped it into froth by repeatedly pouring it from pot to cup and back again. Sometimes they used a beater or stir-stick.

The cacao drinks differed from those familiar today. First and foremost the chocolate was bitter, not sweet. To improve the flavor, Mesoamericans added ground-up chili peppers, vanilla, and other accents. Honey or flower nectar served as sweetener in the absence of sugar. Texture and color were also important. Annatto seeds, for instance, turned the drink as red as blood, and the mixture played an important role in Mexica religious ritual. When it came to everyday use, Mayans often thickened their chocolate with atole, their traditional corn gruel.

The Mexica, unlike the Maya, confined *cacahuatl* use to royalty, priests, honored warriors, and successful merchants. Those invited to drink chocolate did so in situations heavy with ritual significance, as when leaders and warriors gath-

Cacao pods ripening on a tree

ered after to a banquet to commiserate over chocolate and tobacco.

As the Mexica lived in highlands too cool for cacao agriculture, they demanded it as tribute from those they conquered. They also imported it from Mayan regions farther south. A typical Mayan farmer carried his beans via canoe or lugged them on his back in a large basket held in place by a strap across his forehead. Merchants bought the beans at markets and, using human porters, carried the product into Mexica lands or to rendezvous with South American merchants and Caribbean traders.

Cacao beans were so valuable that the Mexica paid workers with beans. A list made after the Spanish arrived priced a turkey hen at one hundred cacao beans. Ripe avocados and large tomatoes went for one bean each. According to Mexica accounts, unscrupulous types counterfeited the currency by treating ordinary beans to look like cacao.

New Agri-Cultures

Early European explorers and colonists recognized the Indians' gifts for exploiting plants. Europeans—especially in North America—often survived only because Native Americans convinced them to eat and grow unfamiliar foods like maize and squash. Over time, however, the descendants of those Europeans forgot or glossed over the achievements in both agriculture and the uses of wild plants.

The Native American achievement with plants has stood the test of time. Since 1492, no one has discovered a single native plant good for food or anything else that one pre-Columbian people or another did not use first.

Partial List of Native American Non-Meat Foods

acorn	passion fruit
amaranth	peanut
avocado	pecan
black bean	pepper
black walnut	pineapple
blueberry	pinion nut
cashew (nut and fruit)	popcorn
cassava	potato
chicle (gum)	prickly pear
chili pepper	pumpkin
chocolate	quinoa
gooseberry	squash
hickory nut	string bean
kidney bean	sunflower seed
Jerusalem artichoke	sweet potato
lima bean	tomato
maize	vanilla
maple syrup	zucchini
papaya	

Chapter Five:
Rubber Balls and Khipus

For generations, history books taught that European technical superiority explained how small numbers of European conquistadors and colonists overwhelmed native peoples. Often advanced technology was seen as an extension of a European civilization superior in breeding, faith, morality, and every other virtue.

Recent research has shattered these old perceptions. Archaeologists, anthropologists, and other specialists now see pre-Columbian Americans as creating and refining technologies that allowed cultures to master whole landscapes, expand societies in new directions, and explore new intellectual and religious horizons.

No one knows the true name of the desert farming people who once lived around present-day Phoenix, Arizona. The Pima, their probable descendants, may have given them the name archaeologists use: Hohokam, or "the ancestors."

The Hohokam migrated from Mexico into basins formed by the Salt and Gila Rivers. Between AD 800 and 1000, the Hohokam expanded their simple irrigation works into an extensive system of ten-foot-deep waterways lined with plaster that not only carried water long distances but also to farms at higher elevations. In its day the Hohokam water system—constructed without iron tools or the convenience of wheeled carts—compared to the irrigation works of ancient Old World civilizations.

Hohokam crafts, meanwhile, rivaled the canals for sophistication. In addition to jewelry and textiles, Hohokam artisans invented a hallmark red-on-buff pottery that is prized by collectors today.

The Maya, too, faced obstacles to agriculture. It sounds ironic on the surface. After all, many Classic Era cities were built in a rain forest, and we tend to think of the rain forest as fertile and, well, rainy. On the contrary, however, rain forest soil is poor. The nutrients circulating in the ecosystem are carried above ground, in the plant and animal life—at least one of the reasons why tree roots crawl along the surface rather than clawing down into the soil as they do in many temperate regions.

Conditions in the Yucatan also affected the supply of water for growing crops. A lengthy dry season and occasional droughts made it imperative for Mayan farmers to save enough water to get them through periods without rain. But the limestone in the ground allowed water to sink so deep it was hard to dig wells. The surface water held in lakes and swamps, meanwhile, was high in salt—and salt damages most human crops, maize included.

Mayan engineering solved many of the problems for a time. *Ahaws* organized the construction of reservoirs to hold water and mazes of trenches to move it around. Laborers sank limestone paving that walled off the salt collected in lake beds from the fresh rainwater at the surface.

Technology may have bumped up against natural limitations, however. When the Classic Era polities remained small, farmers using the slash-and-burn system allowed used patches of land to recover while they farmed another cut out of the forest. But slash-and-burn became more difficult to sustain as the population grew. More people needed more food, and to grow more food, farmers needed more land. Fields once left to regenerate were plowed until exhausted and useless. Needing every inch of arable land, farmers built terraces on hillsides, a strategy that worked until erosive rains washed the soil away.

To what extent Mayan farming practices contributed to the Classic Maya's sudden disappearance remains a matter of debate. If agriculture did lead to problems, however, the Maya would have plenty of company in history. The ancient Greeks and modern Chinese eroded their hillsides; and a lack of respect for drought cycles turned the Great Plains into the Dust Bowl of the 1930s.

Irrigation and Terrace Farming

The peoples of coastal Peru used irrigation thousands of years ago, when the Norte Chico mound-builders irrigated cotton and food crops in the coastal desert. But the farmers in the Andes faced a different set of problems. The mountains rose up from the coast like a steep wall. Plateaus provided flat land suitable for farming. But the mountain terrain limited the amount available and the cold, dry conditions at the higher elevations made a great deal of it unsuitable for anything but potatoes, quinoa, and grazing herds of llamas.

The solution? A system of stairstep terraces built on the mountainsides. Crops grew on narrow strips of soil—often just a few yards wide—held in place by terraces. Water flowing down the mountain collected there for use by plants or was held in ditch-like reservoirs dug by farmers.

The terrace system allowed an Andean farming village to grow a variety of plants, with each crop sewn at an altitude with appropriate rainfall, temperature, and sunlight. For example, a group of farmers might grow potatoes, a hearty tuber called oca, and tarwi, a bean that thrives in bad soil, near their highland homes. At the same time, they had rights to farm terraces thousands of feet and a weeks' journey down the mountain. There they planted maize and beans and perhaps harvested the sweet seeds—today called the ice cream bean—from pacay trees.

Andean farmers boosted their harvests and improved their soil by using fertilizers. Nitrogen-rich guano, or bird droppings, was mined from the beach and from offshore islands where it had accumulated for millennia. Anchovies fished out of the Humboldt Current provided a renewable source of fertilizer along the Peruvian coast. New England peoples, meanwhile, buried a salmon head in a milpa mound to feed growing plants.

The most powerful of the Andean societies, the Inca, inherited terrace-building technology developed over centuries by other mountain peoples. By combining the crop diversity afforded by terrace farming with planning and a storage system, the Inca secured a food supply that powered their economy—and the system of conquest and coercion they used to create the Western Hemisphere's largest empire.

The Inca enter history as rulers of a village called Cuzco in the early thirteenth century. In the late 1300s, the Inca king, named Viracocha or Viracocha Inca, set about conquering his neighbors, and Cuzco became the seat of a growing kingdom. The drama of conquest reached its climax when, in 1438, Viracocha Inca's son dispatched a rival kingdom and took the name Pachakuti, "He who remakes the world."

What we know of Pachakuti's reign comes from oral histories taken down by the Spanish long after.

He did begin to remake his world. Pachakuti ordered thousands of male subjects to haul and work stone, dig ditches, build buildings, and do all the other labor necessary to transform Cuzco into a capital worthy of his people.

Each of Cuzco's paved streets had a channel in the middle that carried away waste—a contrast to the appalling filth on European streets, where people dumped body waste, garbage, dead animals, amputated limbs, and anything else they did not want in the house. The walls of great ceremonial buildings were made of stone blocks. Masons shaped them with stone tools to fit together so well that no mortar was necessary to hold the blocks in place. Homes, temples, palaces, and storehouses and sheds for every kind of good filled out the cityscape. The greatest of the sacred buildings, the *Coricancha* or Temple of the Sun, stood behind a wall fifteen feet (four-and-a-half meters) high and was filled with gold objects.

Pachakuti's successor Topa Inca continued to expand Tawantinsuyu, "the land of the four quarters." From Cuzco, located in the center, a mere 40,000 Inca governed an empire that stretched from Ecuador through Bolivia to Chile and Argentina and may have included 10 million people.

TEMPLE OF CUSCO.

A hand-colored woodcut of a nineteenth century reproduction depicting the Incan Temple of the Sun in Cuzco, Peru, circa the 1500s

rraforming

Many consider the Amazonian rain forest synonymous with the idea of a pristine wilderness. In the past generation, however, some archaeologists and anthropologists have proposed that Native Americans engineered the landscape to such a degree that vast regions of so-called wilderness were actually managed by human beings.

Author Charles Mann described the practice as *terraforming*, a concept familiar to science-fiction fans. Terraforming, as Mann used it, refers to a technology—or rather, a series of interrelated technologies—employed to remake a part of the Earth for human benefit. In Mann's book *1491*, botanical anthropologist Charles R. Clement said rain forest Indians transformed the Amazon Basin into enormous food-rich orchards—his word—by planting favored species of trees that provided nuts, fruit, oils, and other products still found in abundance today.

As part of their work, pre-Columbian terraformers created a tool that remade the earth under their feet. Terra preta, or dark earth, is a fertile and productive type of black or brown soil found in parts of the Amazon. A terra preta layer often is a foot or two deep, though thicker deposits exist. Broken pottery is mixed into the soil layer.

Unlike normal tropical soil, terra preta contains rich organic matter and a bevy of nutrients, including the phosphorus and nitrogen essential for good plant growth. It may also be home to swarms of microorganisms that contribute to soil health.

Terra preta's secret weapon may be its immense amounts of carbon. Nutrients bound to carbon aren't washed away as easily by rain. Natural fertilizers like dead fish, food waste, and night soil (human excrement) stay put for use by plants.

Investigators believe that Amazonian farmers added carbon through the slash-and-char process. During slash-and-char, a farmer partially burns organic matter—wood or garbage, for instance. This creates carbon-rich charcoal that can be broken up and mixed into dirt. By essentially mining the huge amounts of carbon locked into trees, and then adding pottery pieces to encourage good air and water circulation, Amazonian farmers re-engineered bad rain forest soil into good.

Though not averse to using force, the Inca often incorporated new lands into the empire through a combination of pressure and diplomacy. Weaker kingdoms, seeing no alternatives to Inca rule, often gave in.

Textiles on the Rise

Inca technological innovations marched beyond agriculture into fields like government and transportation. Officials traveled to the far-flung lands to carry out the emperor's wishes. Assistants, what we might call bureaucrats, went along to conduct the day-to-day business of running the empire.

The Inca added to smaller roads built by earlier Andean societies and created an extensive highway network 19,000 miles (30,577 kilometers) long. Roads allowed armies to pass, merchants to haul goods, messengers to carry orders, and subject peoples to send tribute in the form of alpaca wool, fish shells, or anything else the Inca rulers wished.

One of the products most in demand was cotton textiles, another ancient Andean technology.

Coastal peoples had woven cotton at least since the times of the Norte Chico farmers. The puffy-headed plant provided the fabric most common in the lowlands. Andeans traded for cotton clothes, though they also had access to wool from the llama, alpaca, and the wild vicuña. As an industry, textile manufacturing was second only to agriculture in the Inca economy; whole villages devoted their labor to it.

But textiles meant far more in Andean culture than the raw material for clothing. Textiles were an art form and could be symbols of prestige on a par with precious metals and jade.

"[T]heir role in Andean societies as carriers of meaning and power is different from anything else I know," said William J. Conklin of Washington D.C.'s Textile Museum.

Nobles and other members of the elite wore the finest weaves decorated with rare feathers, gold and silver, and vivid designs made with colorful dyes. Incan law, meanwhile, mandated that individuals wear the traditional designs of their ethnic group in order to be easily identified.

High-quality *cumbi* cloth was the most valuable of the cotton weaves. The elite burned *cumbi* as an offering to the gods, and Inca officials sometimes gave *cumbi* as a gift to the leaders of groups being incorporated into Tawantinsuyu. Gift-giving, in such cases, was an alternative to bloodshed, and the *cumbi* a small price to pay for a promise of obedience.

Textile technology provided a variety of other cloth types, from rough fiber used for blankets to a tightly-woven fabric strong enough to turn a sword blow.

Cotton grew in strains of red and other colors. But Andean cultures, like those in Mesoamerica and elsewhere, excelled in the use of natural dyes.

Pre-Columbian Americans exploited varied natural sources for dye. In the Amazon, Indians used nuts of the brazilwood tree for red and purple. A type of corn grown in New England provided red, while several peoples used achiote, a seed, as a source of yellow and red-yellow.

One of the most valuable dyes came from the insides of a cactus-dwelling insect. Cochineal dye, from the female cochineal, was used for crimson, red, and yellow. Farmers in Oaxaca maintained cochineal farms to guarantee a supply. Mexica kings demanded it as tribute.

After the Spanish Conquest, cochineal became one of the New World's most valuable exports. In addition to revolutionizing women's fashion, cochineal dye provided the color for the Royal Canadian Mounted Police uniform and the distinctive red coats of the British Army.

The Khipu: Textile-Based Communication

The central role of textiles in Andean life also led to the creation of a textile-based form of communication. The *khipu* was a system of knotted strings the Inca used as a record-keeping system to track goods, manpower, and the other logistical concerns. But *khipu* technology predated the Inca—archaeologists have found *khipu* from the ninth century. If a string object unearthed at Caral in the Norte Chico turns out to be an early *khipu*, it would move its invention back to perhaps 2000 or 2500 BC.

A *khipu* consists of a cord of varying length that may hold anywhere from dozens to a thousand strings. Knots tied along the strings—and secondary knotted strings branching off from the primary strings—create patterns. Those patterns, combined with the color of the string and other factors, allowed a person to "read" information on the *khipu* with their fingers.

For a long time scholars thought the *khipu* system was used solely for accounting. And many *khipu*, it seems, had that function. In recent years, however, scholars studying the *khipu* have investigated whether the Inca used *khipu* as a form of knot-based writing unique in world culture.

Resolving the question means overcoming one major obstacle, however. No one can read a *khipu*. As Harvard anthropologist and *khipu* scholar Gary Urton put it, "The Spaniards were bewildered by them. Four hundred years later, we aren't much better off."

Urton and others continue to search archives from the colonial era for a translation of a *khipu* into Spanish. Such a document would allow them to unlock the *khipu* system and understand what Andean peoples recorded with the device.

Rubber: Balls But No Tires

Clothes made from New World strains of cotton are worn around the world. But another technology had an impact perhaps equal to cotton shirts, maize, and potatoes: rubber.

The Olmec—the "people from the land of rubber"—probably used rubber as early as 1600 BC. It may in fact be even more ancient. To obtain rubber, Mesoamericans harvested the sap of the Panama rubber tree (*Castilla elastica*) and, less often, the guayule (*Parthenium argentatum*). Amazonians used it, too, though they relied on the Para rubber tree (*Hevea brasiliensis*), the species that later became the foundation of the world's commercial rubber industry.

Craftsmen worked rubber by heating the sap and mixing it with various substances to give it extra bounce. Processing rubber was work intensive, to say the least. A cooker had to keep it over a fire and continually add fresh sap to the rubbery blob until it was ready. South American peoples used rubber to make waterproof cloaks and form-fitting boots. Anyone who wanted a pair of rubber boots immersed his or her feet in raw rubber and, it seems, exposed the boot—with one's foot inside—to the heat.

Rubber, specifically the rubber ball, also played an important role in Mesoamerican cultures.

The Mesoamerican ballgame, as it is usually called, may have predated the Olmec. What little we know about it comes from its portrayal in art and of the ball courts found in almost all of the major Mesoamerican ruins. Probably a ritual form played on the city ball courts re-enacted scenes from history and religion, with the losing side pre-determined and destined to die as human sacrifices. At other times, teams may have battled in competitive games for high stakes—life, treasure, and glory. Scenes in art also suggest ordinary people played ball sports for fun.

Players chosen for important games on the ball court may have arrived in colorful headdresses and jewelry, even in one of the valuable jaguar skins esteemed in Mesoamerican culture. Drumming accompanied their entrance and kept up during the contest. This presentation was for show, however. While playing the game the athletes wore little more than pads on their hips and (perhaps) knees, a leather or wicker girdle, and a loin cloth or skirt.

Rules varied by region and time, but many forms of the ballgame were dangerous. The rubber ball in some versions was as large as a volleyball and so heavy that virtually no player escaped a game without bruises. The court, meanwhile,

Sap flows from fresh scores in a rubber tree. The foam is discarded and the liquid is boiled.

had plaster or stone floors. Perhaps not surprisingly, players sometimes suffered broken bones or even death from internal injuries.

The I-shaped court had end zones bracketing a midfield with brightly-painted walls along each side. Teams perhaps scored points by advancing the ball into the opposing end zone. The Maya, particularly those in the north, played a variation with a vertical ring set into the wall. A team putting the ball through the ring seems to have won automatically, regardless of points scored up until then. When this rare event took place, the player may have received the clothes of the opposing team's fans. Mayan artwork suggests the losing team's supporters fled the stadium rather than waiting to be stripped.

Rubber plantations spread across the tropics in the wake of the Columbian Exchange. By the nineteenth century, industrialized countries needed it for machinery and for tires on automobiles and trucks. Mesoamericans, ironically, never used the wheel. Nevertheless, the popular belief that New World peoples never envisioned the wheel is untrue. Archaeologists digging at Tres Zapotes, a city-ceremonial center at the western edge of the Olmec homeland, discovered animal figurines alongside painted clay discs. Tubes for fitting on the clay wheels ran through the front and rear paws. Others have been discovered elsewhere in Mexico. In addition, the Maya used a round limestone roller to pave paths and roadways.

Why Mesoamericans ignored such a useful technology will never be known. One theory holds that the wheel presented no obvious use to people lacking horses or oxen to pull vehicles. Furthermore, the Mesoamerican landscape—whether the swampy Olmec homeland or the Mayan cities hacked out of rain forest—was hostile to road-building, and wheels need roads to roll on.

Travel By Water

Waterways, however, provided pre-Columbian Americans with an enormous alternative highway system. They fashioned several kinds of craft for use in travel, trade, and their own explorations.

Canoes originated as dugouts, a watercraft made by hollowing out a tree trunk and shaping the front and back to slice through water. Arawak and Carib peoples in the Caribbean used dugouts in everyday life as well as on their long-distance migrations. Choctaws farther north navigated the coast of the Gulf of Mexico in dugouts. In the Pacific Northwest, peoples like the Kwakiutls and Suquamish built forty-foot dugouts from red cedar and used the boats for whaling.

Boat builders in northern climes, lacking the giant tree species best for dugouts, created a wooden frame resembling a rib cage and held together by tough pine or spruce tree roots, or with glue. The frame was then covered with lightweight, waterproof bark—birch was popular—and waterproofed using a sealant of heated tree resin. Not only did the birchbark canoe handle well, repairs were easy. If a boat developed a problem, those using it simply ducked into the forest for fresh wood, bark, or resin.

Canoes could be smallish one- or two-person craft most familiar to us today. But pre-Columbian traders built versions more than twenty feet long, four-feet wide, and capable of hauling 1,000 pounds (454 kilograms).

The frequency of contacts between trading canoes and European explorers suggests widespread canoe use. Seafaring traders were the first Inca to meet Spanish conquistadors. Columbus may have made Spain's first contact with the Maya in 1502 when his brother Bartholomew met a dugout canoe at a village off the coast of Honduras. The boat was one of the larger kind. Twenty-five sailors in dyed cotton clothing handled the cargo while their women and children waited in the shade under an awning.

Arctic peoples living in a treeless landscape developed their own watercraft using driftwood for a frame and substituting animal skins for bark. By covering the boat's open top except for a narrow place to sit, they invented the kayak. Lightweight and maneuverable, the kayak allowed hunters to navigate sea ice as well as open water in search of prey. A hunter literally wore his boat. If it capsized—a likely enough possibility if confronting a whale—the hunter remained in his seat and with a well-practiced motion flipped the kayak rightside-up.

The larger, open umiak was also made using animal skin. Umiaks, unlike kayaks, provided hauling power, and could act as a freight boat or as a whaling boat for a team of harpoon-armed hunters. Because an umiak was lightweight, families or hunters could also drag it onto the shore for use as a shelter.

People sailed reed boats on Andes lakes. An ancient technology, reed boats appeared independently in the Middle East and Africa. The Aymara along Lake Titicata fashioned the totora, a distinctive craft made from the reeds of a local water plant also called totora. Taking the idea further, the pre-Incan Kot-suña, or Uros, people also built man-made reed islands that are still in use today.

In many areas of the Amazon, people still live a lifestyle that has changed little since pre-Columbian times. The dugout canoe continues to be an important and efficient means of transportation.

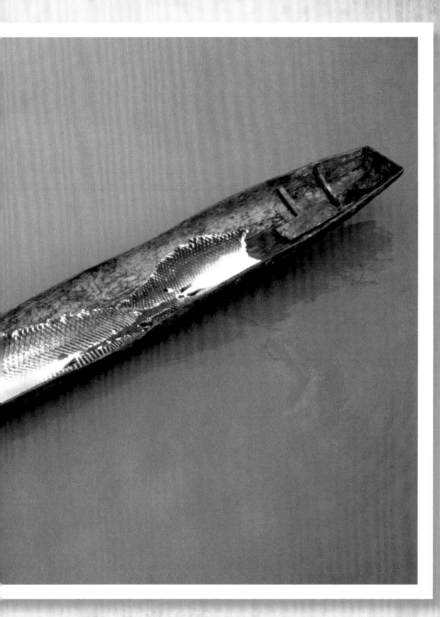

Early Documentation

For most pre-Columbian cultures, knowledge of technology—and everything else—was passed along primarily via oral communication. That might mean person-to-person teaching, poetry, stories, songs, ritual language, or active participation in activities like hunting or baking with elders on hand to mentor. But permanent forms of storing information did exist: the *khipu*, for instance, and calendars, and of course art, whether pictographs on desert walls or images on pottery. Mesoamericans, however, also created the kind of information storage system most familiar to modern people—writing.

Ancient American Calendars

The Maya and Mexica kept formal calendars. The Maya haab and Mexica *xiuhpohualli*, each a regular calendar of days, had eighteen months of twenty days each, for 360 days. The five days left over the Maya consigned to a short nineteenth month. For the Mexica, no gods watched over this "useless filling" of days, and parents hoped their children would not be born then.

Modern astronomers know the actual solar year is about a quarter of a day over 365 days. Our leap year accounts for the discrepancy and puts the calendar back on track. Mesoamericans also recognized the problem and allowed for it.

Both the Mayans and the Mexica kept a second 260-day sacred calendar. Every fifty-two years, the calendars ended on the same day, and at the end the Mexica observed the "binding of the years." Since they believed the world would end at the close of a fifty-two year "century," the approach of such a date was a tense time. When it passed, the Mexica observed a period of celebration and renewal that featured the lighting of sacred fires and a procession to Tenochtitlan's main temple for an important human sacrifice. Another calendar, the long count, stretched back into the distant past. Archaeologists fix the exact date it begins as August 11 in the year 3114 BC. The long count provided a logical, precise system for recording historical events, and dates on Mayan monuments used the long count system.

As far as we know, three ancient societies invented writing without any influence from another culture: the Chinese, the Sumerians of the Tigris-Euphrates river valley, and the Maya, with the Egyptians a possible fourth. (Note, however, that some linguists believe Olmec or Zapotec writing preceded that of the Maya.) Early versions of Mayan glyphs on murals in Guatemala date to after 300 BC.

Mayan writing often appears in two vertical rows. The top row is read left-to-right, then the second row left-to-right, and so on. Though the Maya carved glyphs into stone and wood and painted glyphs on pottery, they also wrote—or, rather, painted—on amate, a kind of paper made from the inner bark of the wild fig tree. Page sizes varied from about 8-by-3.5 inches to 9.75-by-5 inches (20.3-by-8.9 centimeters to 24.8-by-12.7 centimeters). Once the pages were fastened together with gum, the book, called a codex by modern scholars, opened like a screen or folded map. The longest known codex had 112 pages and stretched over 23.5 feet (7.2 meters).

Thousands of codices probably existed prior to 1492, but next to none survived the Spanish Conquest. Tropical humidity and mold claimed an unknown number, but many were destroyed by Diego de Landa, a Franciscan monk assigned to the Yucatan to convert the Maya to Catholicism. Landa instigated an attempt at the wholesale destruction of Mayan culture, starting with the codices:

> These people also made use of certain characters or letters, with which they wrote in their books their ancient affairs and their sciences. . . . We found a great number of books in these characters, and, as they contained nothing in which there was not to be seen superstition and lies of the devil, we burned them all, which they regretted to an amazing degree and caused them affliction.

These Mayan glyphs carved on the back of a stela, or a standing stone slab, at the Copan ruins in Honduras, tell the story of their civilization.

In another of history's ironies, the surviving portions of Landa's report on the Maya contributed greatly to our understanding of the fifteenth-century Maya's religion, culture, and written and spoken languages. The campaign he started, meanwhile, continued until 1697, when the Spanish conquered Tayasal, the last holdout Mayan kingdom, and burned its written records.

Only three whole codices still exist. Each is named after the city where it resides—Madrid, Dresden, and Paris. An eleven-page fragment of a fourth codex, the Grolier, appeared in the 1970s, but its authenticity is uncertain. Archaeologists have also fished a handful of codices out of tombs, but all are either too damaged to open or have been reduced to flecks of matter.

The Mexica also kept codices on bark paper and animal skins, though the few surviving codices from before the Spanish Conquest contain mostly pictures instead of writing. Though the Mexica written language was simpler than that of the Maya, it allowed them to keep land ownership records and family histories.

History in Flux

It is always tempting for historians and readers alike to compare Native American accomplishments with those of the Europeans. And, indeed, a widespread reconsideration of four centuries of history along those lines has endowed Native American accomplishments with a degree of respect unheard-of in previous generations. At the same time, the eclipse of Native American culture by Europeans is being increasingly seen as less a victory of superior European culture and more as a conquest by European diseases that left populations—including those of the Mexica and Inca—too devastated to defend themselves.

One benefit of taking a revised view of the past is to see what pre-Columbian peoples did on their own terms, without comparisons. It allows us to understand that an event like the domestication of maize altered human history before 1492, and that what came after, while part of the story, is far from the whole story. What happened at Chaco Canyon or Cahokia is seen not as behind the Old World developments of the year 1000 but as an alternative path for human beings that included all the complex beliefs, baffling decisions, and soaring ideas found in every society.

The story, when told that way, is no longer simple. No human story can be. And in the end, the real breakthrough may come when the human beings of the Western Hemisphere are integrated into the narrative of world history.

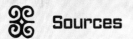 **Sources**

CHAPTER ONE:
A Past Evolving Over Time

p. 11-13, "And when we . . ." Bernal Díaz, *The Conquest of New Spain,* trans. John M. Cohen (New York: Penguin, 1963), 214.

CHAPTER TWO:
Solving Prehistory's Mysteries

p. 23, "Clovis points . . ." Public Broadcasting System, "America's Stone Age Explorers." Transcript of broadcast. *Nova,* November 9, 2004.

p. 28, "Our findings . . ." University of Copenhagen, "The Voyage to America." Press release, April 3, 2008.

CHAPTER THREE:
Forgotten Cities

p. 34, "The people who built . . ." Northern Illinois University, "Archaeologists Shed New Light on Americas' Earliest Known Civilization." News release, December 2004.

p. 37, "The Wari were . . ." Andrew Curry, "Trophy Skulls and Beer." *Archaeology* 63 (January/February 2010): 43.

p. 43-44, "With apparent disregard . . ." Ignacio Bernal, *The Olmec World* (Berkeley, CA: University of California Press, 1969), 70.

p. 49, "Someone who was already important . . ." Harold Henderson, "The Rise and Fall of the Mound Peoples," *Chicago Reader,* June 29, 2000.

p. 53, "The women never show injury . . ." George Pawlaczyk, "Human Sacrifice! Archaeologist Creates Stir with New Book on Cahokia Mounds," *Belleville News-Democrat,* August 9, 2009.

CHAPTER FOUR:

Harvest

p. 57, "catastrophic and bountiful . . ." Alfred Crosby, *The Columbian Exchange: Biological and Cultural Consequences of 1492* (Westport, CN: Praeger, 2003), XX.

p. 60, "arguably man's first . . ." Charles C. Mann, *1491: New Revelations of the Americas Before Columbus* (New York: Vintage, 2005), 218.

p. 60, "To get corn . . ." Ibid.

p. 60, "Where [maize] flourished . . ." Michael D. Coe, *America's First Civilization: Discovering the Olmec* (New York: American Heritage Publishing, 1968), 26.

p. 63, "As to the meals . . ." Sylvanus G. Morley and George W. Brainerd, *The Ancient Maya* (Stanford, CA: Stanford University Press, 1968), 176.

p. 67, "gold and silver . . ." Thomas A. Joyce, *South American Archaeology* (New York: G. P. Putnam's Sons, 1912), 209.

CHAPTER FIVE:

Rubber Balls and Khipus

p. 83, "[T]heir role in Andean societies . . ." Charles C. Mann, "Unraveling Khipu's Secrets," *Science,* August 12, 2005, 1009.

p. 85, "The Spaniards were bewildered . . ." Ibid.

p. 93, "These people . . ." Morley and Brainerd, *The Ancient Maya*, 249.

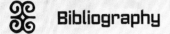

Bibliography

Selected Books

Adams, Richard E. W. *Prehistoric Mesopotamia.* New York: Little, Brown, 2005.

Adovasio, J. M., and Jake Page. *The First Americans.* New York: Random House, 2002.

Bauer, Brian S. *Ancient Cuzco: Heartland of the Inca.* Austin, TX: University of Texas Press, 2004.

Bernal, Ignacio. *The Olmec World.* Berkeley, CA: University of California Press, 1969.

Calloway, Colin G. *One Vast Winter Count: The Native American West Before Louis and Clark.* Lincoln, NE: University of Nebraska Press, 2003.

Chatters, James C. *Ancient Encounters: Kennewick Man and the First Americans.* New York: Touchstone, 2001.

Civitello, Linda. *Cuisine and Culture.* Hoboken, NJ: Wiley and Sons, 2008.

Clendinnen, Inga. *Aztecs.* New York: Cambridge University Press, 1991.

Coe, Michael D. *America's First Civilization: Discovering the Olmec.* New York: American Heritage Publishing, 1968.

Coe, Sophie, and Michael D. Coe. *The True History of Chocolate.* New York: Thames and Hudson, 2007.

Cook, Noble David. *Born to Die: Disease and the New World Conquest, 1492-1650.* New York: Cambridge University Press, 1998.

Covey, R. Alan. *How the Incas Built their Heartland.* Ann Arbor, MI: University of Michigan Press, 2006.

Crosby, Alfred W. *The Columbian Exchange: Biological and Cultural Consequences of 1492.* Westport, CN: Praeger, 2003.

———. *Ecological Imperialism: The Biological Expansion of Europe, 900-1900.* New York: Cambridge University Press, 1986.

De Acosta, Jose. *Natural and Moral History of the Indies.* Edited by Jane E. Mangan. Translated by Frances López-Morillas. Durham, NC: Duke University Press, 2002.

Deloria, Vine, Jr. *Custer Died for Your Sins: An Indian Manifesto.* New York: Macmillan, 1969.

Demarest, Arthur. *The Ancient Maya: The Rise and Fall of a Rainforest Civilization.* New York: Cambridge University Press, 2004.

Diamond, Jared. *Collapse: How Societies Choose or Fail to Succeed.* New York: Penguin, 2005.

Díaz, Bernal. *The Conquest of New Spain.* Translated by John M. Cohen. New York: Penguin, 1963.

Dillehay, Thomas D. *The Settlement of the Americas: A New Prehistory.* New York: Basic Books, 2000.

Fagan, Brian. *The Great Journey: The Peopling of Ancient America.* New York: Thames and Hudson, 1987.

———. *Kingdoms of Gold, Kingdoms of Jade.* New York: Thames and Hudson, 1991.

Fussell, Betty. *The Story of Corn.* New York: Random House, 1992.

Greenfield, Amy Butler. *A Perfect Red: Empire, Espionage, and the Quest for the Color of Desire.* New York: HarperCollins, 2005.

Hancock, J. F. *Plant Evolution and the Origin of Crop Species.* Cambridge, MA: CABI Publishing, 2004.

Hassig, Ross. *War and Society in Ancient Mesoamerica.* Berkeley, CA: University of California Press, 1992.

Hemming, John. *The Conquest of the Incas.* New York: Harcourt, Brace, Jovanovich, 1970.

Hendon, Julia A., and Rosemary A. Joyce, eds. *Mesoamerican Archaeology.* Malden, MA: Blackwell, 2004.

Henige, David. *Numbers from Nowhere: The American Indian Contact Population Debate.* Norman, OK: University of Oklahoma Press, 1998.

Jablonski, Nina G. *The First Americans: The Pleistocene Colonization of the New World.* Berkeley: University of California Press, 2002.

Josephy, Alvin M., Jr., ed. *America in 1492.* New York: Knopf, 1992.

Joyce, Thomas A. *South American Archaeology.* New York: G. P. Putnam's Sons, 1912.

Kiple, Kenneth F. *The Cambridge World History of Human Disease.* New York: Cambridge University Press, 1993.

Kiple, Kenneth F., and Kriemhild Coneé Ornelas. *The Cambridge History of World Food.* New York: Cambridge University Press, 2000.

Knight, Alan. *Mexico: From the Beginning to the Spanish Conquest.* New York: Cambridge University Press, 2002.

Krech III, Shepard. *The Ecological Indian: Myth and History.* New York: W. W. Norton, 1999.

Loadman, John. *Tears of the Tree: The Story of Rubber, a Modern Marvel.* Oxford, England: Oxford University Press, 2005.

Logan, William Bryant. *Oak: The Frame of Civilization.* New York: W. W. Norton, 2005.

Mann, Charles C. *1491: New Revelations of the Americas Before Columbus.* New York: Vintage, 2005.

McGovern, Patrick E. *Uncorking the Past: The Quest for Wine, Beer, and Other Alcoholic Beverages.* Berkeley, CA: University of California Press, 2009.

Meltzer, David J. *First Peoples in a New World: Colonizing Ice Age America.* Berkeley, CA: University of California Press, 2009.

Moerman, Daniel E. *Native American Ethnobotany.* Portland, OR: Timber Press, 1998.

Montgomery, David R. *Dirt: The Erosion of Civilizations.* Berkeley, CA: University of California Press, 2007.

Morley, Sylvanus Griswold, and George W. Brainerd. *The Ancient Maya.* Stanford, CA: Stanford University Press, 1968.

Moseley, Michael E. *The Incas and their Ancestors.* New York: Thames and Hudson, 1992.

National Research Council. *Lost Crops of the Incas.* Washington, DC: National Academy Press, 1989.

Nicholls, Steve. *Paradise Found: Nature in America at the Time of Discovery.* Chicago: University of Chicago Press, 2009.

Paddock, John, ed. *Ancient Oaxaca: Discoveries in Mexican Archaeology and History.* Stanford, CA: Stanford University Press, 1966.

Pauketat, Timothy R. *Ancient Cahokia and the Mississippians.* Cambridge, England: Cambridge University Press, 2004.

———. *Cahokia: Ancient America's Great City on the Mississippi.* New York: Penguin, 2009.

Pauketat, Timothy R., and Thomas E. Emerson, eds. *Cahokia: Domination and Ideology in the Mississippian World.* Lincoln, NE: University of Nebraska Press, 1997.

Pielou, E. C. *After the Ice Age: The Return of Life to Glaciated North America.* Chicago: University of Chicago Press, 1991.

Pool, Christopher A. *Olmec Archaeology and Early Mesoamerica.* New York: Cambridge University Press, 2007.

Reader, John. *Potato: A History of the Propitious Esculent.* New Haven, CT: Yale University Press, 2009.

Roberts, David. *In Search of the Old Ones: Exploring the Anasazi World of the Southwest.* New York: Simon and Schuster, 1996.

Salaman, Redcliffe. *The History and Social Influence of the Potato.* Edited by J. G. Hawkes. New York: Cambridge University Press, 1985.

Schele, Linda, and David Freidel. *A Forest of Kings: The Untold Story of the Ancient Maya.* New York: William Morrow, 1990.

Schlesinger, Victoria. *Animals and Plants of the Ancient Maya.* Austin, TX: University of Texas Press, 2001.

Shaffer, Lynda Norene. *Native Americans Before 1492.* Armonk, NY: M. E. Sharpe, 1992.

Sharer, Robert J., and Loa P. Traxler. *The Ancient Maya.* Stanford, CA: Stanford University Press, 2006.

Silverman, Helaine, ed. *Andean Archaeology.* Malden, MA: Blackwell, 2004.

Silverman, Helaine, and William H. Isbell, eds. *Handbook of South American Archaeology.* New York: Springer, 2008.

Smith, C. Wayne, Javier Betrán, and E. C. A. Runge, eds. *Corn: Origin, History, Technology, and Production.* Hoboken, NJ: Wiley & Sons, 2004.

Smith, Michael E. *The Aztecs.* Malden, MA: Blackwell, 2003.

Smith, Michael E., and Marilyn A. Masson. *The Ancient Civilizations of Mesoamerica: A Reader.* Malden, MA: Blackwell, 2000.

Soustelle, Jacques. *Daily Life of the Aztecs.* Mineola, NY: Dover, 2002.

Staller, John Edward, and Michael Carrasco. *Pre-Columbian Foodways.* New York: Springer, 2010.

Staller, John Edward, Robert H. Tykot, and Bruce F. Benz, eds. *Histories of Maize.* Burlington, MA: Academic Press, 2006.

Stannard, David E. *American Holocaust: Columbus and the Conquest of the New World.* New York: Oxford University Press, 1992.

Sykes, Bryan. *The Seven Daughters of Eve.* New York: W. W. Norton, 2001.

Thomas, Hugh. *Conquest: Montezuma, Cortes, and the Fall of Old Mexico.* New York: Simon and Schuster, 1993.

Thornton, Russell. *American Indian Holocaust and Survival: A Population History Since 1492*. Norman, OK: University of Oklahoma Press, 1988.

Vlasich, James A. *Pueblo Indian Architecture*. Albuquerque, NM: University of New Mexico Press, 2005.

Weatherford, Jack. *Indian Givers: How the Indians of the Americas Transformed the World*. New York: Ballantine Books, 1988.

———. *Native Roots: How the Indians Enriched America*. New York: Crown, 1991.

West, Frederick Hadleigh, ed. *American Beginnings: The Prehistory and Paleoecology of Beringia*. Chicago: University of Chicago Press, 1996.

Wilson, James. *The Earth Shall Weep: A History of Native America*. New York: Atlantic Monthly Press, 2000.

Young-Sánchez, Margaret. *Tiwanaku: Ancestors of the Inca*. Denver, CO: Denver Art Museum, 2004.

Periodicals

Ceci, Lynn. "Fish Fertilizer: A Native North American Practice?" *Science* 188 (April 4, 1975): 26–30.

Cowley, Geoffrey. "The Great Disease Migration." *Newsweek* (Special Issue, Fall/Winter 1991): 54–56.

Curry, Andrew. "Trophy Skulls and Beer." *Archaeology* 63 (January/February 2010): 38–43.

Diamond, Jared. "The Arrow of Disease." *Discover* 13 (October 1992): 64–73.

Eshleman, J. A., Ripan S. Malhi, and David G. Smith. "Mitochondrial DNA Studies of Native Americans: Conceptions and Misconceptions of the Population Prehistory of the Americas." *Evolutionary Anthropology* 12 (2003): 7–18.

Gibbons, Ann. "Monte Verde: Blessed But Not Confirmed." *Science* 275 (February 28, 1997): 1256–57.

Haas, Jonathan, Winifred Creamer, and Alvaro Ruiz. "Dating the Late Archaic Occupation of the Norte Chico Region in Peru." *Nature* 432 (December 23, 2004): 1020–23.

Iltis, Hugh H. "From Teosinte to Maize: The Catastrophic Sexual Transmutation." *Science* 222 (November 25, 1983): 886–894.

Kloor, Keith. "Who Were the Anasazi?" *Archaeology* 62 (November/December 2009): 18, 60.

Largent, Jr., Floyd. "E. James Dixon and the Peopling of the New World." *Mammoth Trumpet* 20 (September 2005): 11–13.

Lawler, Andrew. "Beyond the Family Feud." *Archaeology* 60 (March/April 2007): 18–19.

Mann, Charles C. "Clovis Technology Flowered Briefly and Late, Dates Suggest." *Science* 315 (February 23, 2007): 1067.

———. "Cracking the Khipu Code." *Science* 300 (June 13, 2003): 1650–1651.

———. "Earthmovers of the Amazon." *Science* 287 (February 4, 2000): 786–789.

———. "Oldest Civilization in the Americas Revealed." *Science* 307 (January 7, 2005): 34–35.

————. "The Real Dirt on Rainforest Fertility." *Science* 297 (August 9, 2002): 920–923.

————. "Unraveling Khipu's Secrets." *Science* 309 (August 12, 2005): 1008–1009.

Motamayor, J. C., A. M. Risterucci, P. A. Lopez, C. F. Ortiz, A. Moreno, and C. Lanaud. "Cacao Domestication I: The Origin of the Cacao Cultivated by the Mayas." *Heredity* 89 (2002): 380–386.

Pringle, Heather. "The First Urban Center in the Americas." *Science* 292 (April 27, 2001): 621.

Ramenofsky, Ann F. "Death by Disease." *Archaeology* 45 (March/April 1992): 47–49.

Solis, Ruth Shady, Jonathan Haas, and Winifred Creamer. "Dating Caral, a Preceramic Site in the Supe Valley on the Central Coast of Peru." *Science* 292 (April 27, 2001): 723–26.

Waters, Michael R., and Thomas W. Stafford, Jr. "Redefining the Age of Clovis: Implications for the Peopling of the Americas." *Science* 315 (February 23, 2007): 1122–26.

Online

Achilli, A., U. A. Perego, Claudio M. Bravi, Michael D. Coble, Qing-Peng Kong, Scott R. Woodward, Antonio Salas, Antonio Torroni, and Hans-Jürgen Bandelt. "The Phylogeny of the Four Pan-American MtDNA Haplogroups: Implications for Evolutionary and Disease Studies." *PLoS ONE* 3 (2008). http://www.plosone.org/article/info%3Adoi%2F10.1371%2Fjournal.pone.0001764.

American Association for the Advancement of Science. "Oldest Evidence of City Life in the Americas Reported in *Science*, Early Urban Planners Emerge as Power Players." News release, April 26, 2001. http://www.eurekalert.org/pub_releases/2001-04/AAft-Oeoc-2604101.php.

American Journal of Botany. "The Amazing Maze of Maize Evolution." Press release, October 2, 2009. http://www.eurekalert.org/pub_releases/2009-10/ajob-tam100209.php.

American Society of Agronomy. "Spud Origin Controversy Solved." Press release. *First Science,* May 15, 2007. http://www.firstscience.com/home/news/agriculture/spud-origin-controversy-solved_26323.html.

Associated Press. "Peru, Chile Fight Over Potato's Origin." *USA Today,* May 27, 2008. http://www.usatoday.com/news/world/2008-05-27-peru-chile-potato_N.htm.

Banyasz, Malin Grunberg. "The Neward Earthworks: Ohio's World-Class Archaeological Site." *Archaeology,* October 7, 2009. http://www.archae-ology.org/online/features/hopewell/.

Belsie, Laurent. "Civilization Lost?" *Christian Science Monitor,* January 3, 2002. http://www.csmonitor.com/2002/0103/p11s1-woam.html.

Bensen, Amanda. "A Brief History of Chocolate." *Smithsonian,* March 1, 2008. http://www.smithsonianmag.com/arts-culture/brief-his-tory-of-chocolate.html.

Benson, Elizabeth P. "Dumberton Oaks Conference on the Olmec." Dumberton Oaks Research Library and Collection and the Trustees for Harvard University. October 28–29, 1967. http://www.doaks.org/publica-tions/doaks_online_publications/Olmec.pdf.

Berg, Emmett. "The Lost City of Cahokia: Ancient Tribes of the Mississippi Brought to Life." *Humanities* 25 (September/October 2004). http://www.neh.gov/news/humanities/2004-09/cahokia.html.

Biello, David. "Ancient Stone Weapons Not Ancient Enough to Be Used by First Americans." *Scientific American,* February 22, 2007. http://www.scientificamerican.com/article.cfm?id=ancient-stone-weapons-not-ancient-enough-for-first-americans.

Brahic, Catherine. "Amazon Hides an Ancient Urban Landscape." *New Scientist,* August 29, 2008. http://www.newscientist.com/article/dn14624-amazon-hides-an-ancient-urban-landscape.html?feedId=online-news_rss20.

British Broadcasting Corporation. "'Ancient City Unearthed' in Peru." December 17, 2008. http://news.bbc.co.uk/2/hi/7787053.stm.

————. "The Lost Pyramids of Caral." Transcript of broadcast. *Horizon,* January 31, 2002. http://www.bbc.co.uk/science/horizon/2001/caraltrans.shtml.

————. "The Secret of El Dorado." Transcript of broadcast. *Horizon,* December 19, 2003. http://www.bbc.co.uk/science/horizon/2002/eldoradotrans.shtml.

Cahokia Mounds State Historic Site. http://cahokiamounds.org/.

Casselman, Anne. "Inspired by Ancient Amazonians, a Plan to Convert Trash Into Environmental Treasure." *Scientific American,* May 15, 2007. http://www.scientificamerican.com/article.cfm?id=pyrolyisis-terra-preta-could-eliminate-garbage-generate-oil-carbon-sequestration&page=2.

Chatters, James C. "Kennwick Man." *Newsletter of the American Anthropological Association.* http://www.mnh.si.edu/arctic/html/kennewick_man.html.

Connor, Steve. "DNA Found in Oregon Rewrites the Book on the First Native Americans." *Independent* (UK), April 4, 2008. http://www.independent.co.uk/news/science/dna-found-in-oregon-rewrites-the-book-on-the-first-native-americans-804542.html.

Curry, Andrew. "Pre-Clovis Breakthrough." *Archaeology,* April 3, 2008. http://www.archaeology.org/online/features/coprolites/.

Esty, Amos. "An Interview with Paul S. Martin." *American Scientist,* Undated. http://www.americanscientist.org/bookshelf/pub/an-interview-with-paul-s-martin.

Fagundes, Nelson J. R., Ricardo Kanitz, Roberta Eckert, Ana C. S. Valls, Mauricio R. Bogo, Francisco M. Salzano, David Glenn Smith, Wilson A. Silva, Jr., Marco A. Zago, Andrea K. Ribeiro-dos-Santos, Sidney E. B. Santos, Maria Luiza Petzl-Erler, and Sandro L. Bonatto. "Mitochondrial Population Genomics Supports a Single Pre-Clovis Origin with a Coastal Route for the Peopling of the Americas." *American Journal of Human Genetics* (2008). http://www.familytreedna.com/pdf/Fagundes-et-al.pdf.

Field Museum. "Ancient Brewery Discovered on Mountaintop in Peru." News release, July 27, 2004. http://www.eurekalert.org/pub_releases/2004-07/fm-abd072704.php.

Fleming, Nic. "Archaeologists Push Back Beginning of Civilization in Americas 400 Years." *Telegraph* (UK), December 23, 2004. http://www.telegraph.co.uk/technology/3337503/Archaeologists-push-back-beginning-of-civilization-in-Americas-400-years.html.

Foundation for the Advancement of Mesoamerican Studies. PDFs of the Dresden, Grolier, Madrid, and Paris Codices. Undated. http://www.famsi.org/mayawriting/codices/marhenke.html.

Hall, Stephen S. "Spirits in the Sand." *National Geographic,* March 2010. http://ngm.nationalgeographic.com/2010/03/nasca/hall-text/1.

Hecht, Jeff. "First American Civilization Sprang Up Fast." *New Scientist,* December 22, 2004. http://www.newscientist.com/article/dn6829-first-american-civilisation-sprang-up-fast.html.

———. "First Americans Left Fossil Stools in Cave Latrine." *New Scientist,* April 3, 2008. http://www.newscientist.com/article/dn13586-first-americans-left-fossil-stools-in-cave-latrine.html.

Henderson, Harold. "The Rise and Fall of the Mound Peoples." *Chicago Reader,* June 29, 2000. http://www.chicagoreader.com/chicago/the-rise-and-fall-of-the-mound-people/Content?oid=902673.

Hey, Jody. "On the Number of New World Founders: A Population Genetic Portrait of the Peopling of the Americas." *PLoS Biology* 3 (2005). http://www.plosbiology.org/article/info:doi/10.1371/journal.pbio.0030193.

Kelly, Robert L., and Lawrence C. Todd. "Coming into the Country: Early Paleoindian Hunting and Mobility." *American Antiquity* 53 (1988). http://www.jstor.org/pss/281017.

King, Robert. "In Search of the First Americans: A Story of Deepening Complexity." U.S. Department of the Interior, Bureau of Land Management, undated. http://www.blm.gov/ak/st/en/prog/culture/1st_americans.html.

Kitchen, Andrew, Michael M. Miyamoto, and Connie J. Mulligan. "A Three-Stage Colonization Model for the Peopling of the Americas." *PLoS One* 3 (February 13, 2008). http://www.plosone.org/article/info%3Adoi%2F10.1371%2Fjournal.pone.0001596.

Krech III, Shepard. "Paleoindians and the Great Pleistocene Die-Off." Nature Transformed, National Humanities Center, January 6, 2010. http://nationalhumanitiescenter.org/tserve/nattrans/ntecoindian/essays/pleistocene.htm.

LeCount, Lisa J. "Like Water for Chocolate: Feasting and Political Ritual Among the Late Classic Maya at Xunantunich, Belize." *American Anthropologist* 103 (2001). http://www.jstor.org/pss/684122.

Lentz, David L., Mary DeLand Pohl, José Luis Alvarado, Somayeh Tarighat, and Robert Bye. "Sunflower (*Helianthus annuus* L.) as a Pre-Columbian Domesticate in Mexico." *PNAS* 105 (April 29, 2008). http://www.pnas.org/content/105/17/6232.full.

Llana, Sara Miller. "Last of a Breed Who Make Boats out of Reeds." *Christian Science Monitor,* February 25, 2009. http://www.csmonitor.com/The-Culture/2009/0225/last-of-a-breed-who-make-boats-out-of-reeds.

Lovgren, Stefan. "Clovis People Not First Americans, Study Finds." *National Geographic,* February 23, 2007. http://news.nationalgeographic.com/news/2007/02/070223-first-americans.html

————. "Earliest Known American Settlers Harvested Seaweed." *National Geographic,* May 8, 2008. http://news.nationalgeographic.com/news/2008/05/080508-first-americans.html.

Meltzer, David J. "Coming to America." *Discover,* October 1993. http://discovermagazine.com/1993/oct/comingtoamerica275.

Meltzer, David J., Donald K. Grayson, Gerardo Ardila, Alex W. Barker, Dena F. Dincauze, C. Vance Haynes, Fracisco Mena, Lautaro Nunez, and Dennis J. Stanford. "On the Pleistocene antiquity of Monte Verde, Southern Chile." *American Antiquity* 62 (October 1997): 659–663. http://www.jstor.org/pss/281884.

Mercyhurst College. "Underwater Exploration Seeks Evidence of Early Americans." Press release, July 9, 2009. http://www.eurekalert.org/pub_releases/2009-07/mc-ues070909.php.

Miller, Kenneth. "Showdown at the O. K. Caral." *Discover,* September 9, 2005. http://discovermagazine.com/2005/sep/showdown-at-caral.

Moseley, Michael E. "The Maritime Foundations of Andean Civilization: An Evolving Hypothesis." Hall of Ma'at. August 10, 2004. http://www.hallofmaat.com/modules.php?name=Articles&file=article&sid=85.

Moseman, Andrew. "Ancient Clovis Toolbox: Were Prehistoric Nomads DIYers?" *Popular Mechanics,* March 10, 2009. http://www.popularmechanics.com/blogs/science_news/4307990.html.

Nash, Donna. "Digging at Peru's Cerro Mejía." *Archaeology,* December 4, 2009. http://www.archaeology.org/online/features/cerro_mejia/.

National Science Foundation. "Scientists Find Earliest 'New World' Writings in Mexico." Press release, December 5, 2002. http://www.nsf.gov/od/lpa/news/02/pr0297.htm.

————. "Scientists Trace Corn Ancestry from Ancient Grass to Modern Crop." Press release, May 27, 2005. http://www.nsf.gov/news/news_summ.jsp?org=NSF&cntn_id=104207&preview=false.

Northern Illinois University. "Archaeologists Say Peru Was Home to the Americas' Oldest Pyramids, Cities." News release, April 26, 2001. http://www.niu.edu/pubaffairs/presskits/wcjo/release.html.

————. "Archaeologists Shed New Light on Americas' Earliest Known Civilization." News release, 2004. http://www.niu.edu/PubAffairs/RELEASES/2004/dec/peru.shtml.

————. "Exploring the Americas' Earliest Known Civilization." Press kit, undated. http://www.niu.edu/pubaffairs/presskits/peru/photos.html.

O'Hehir, Andrew. "Sacrificial Virgins of the Mississippi." *Salon,* August 6, 2009. http://www.salon.com/books/review/2009/08/06/cahokia/index.html.

Paleoindian Database of the Americas. http://pidba.utk.edu/main.htm.

Parfit, Michael. "The Dawn of Humans: Who Were the First Americans?" *National Geographic* (December 2000). http://ngm.nationalgeographic.com/ngm/0012/feature3/fulltext.html.

Pauketat, Timothy R. "America's First Pastime." *Archaeology* 62 (September/October 2009). http://www.archaeology.org/0909/abstracts/pastime.html.

Pawlaczyk, George. "Human Sacrifice! Archaeologist Creates Stir With New Book on Cahokia Mounds." *Belleville News-Democrat,* August 9, 2009. http://www.bnd.com/2009/08/09/875703/human-sacrifice-archae-ologist.html.

Peeples, Lynn. "The Origin of Rubber Boots." *Scientific American,* August 21, 2009. http://www.scientificamerican.com/article.cfm?id=origin-rubber-boots-amazonian-indians-goodyear.

Perego, Ugo, Alessandro Achilli, Norman Angehofer, Matteo Accetturo, Maria Pala, Anna Olivieri, Baharak Hooshiar Kashani, Kathleen H. Ritchie, Rosaria Scozzari, Qing-Peng Kong, Natalie M. Myres, Antonio Salas, Ornella Semino, Hans-Jürgen Bandelt, Scott R. Woodward, and Antonio Torroni. "Distinctive Paleo-Indian Migration Routes from Beringia Marked by Two Rare mtDNA Haplogroups." *Current Biology* 19 (January 13, 2009). http://www.ncbi.nlm.nih.gov/pubmed/19135370.

Pringle, Heather. "The Plague That Never Was." *New Scientist,* July 20, 1996. http://www.newscientist.com/article/mg15120394.300-the-plague-that-never-was.html.

Proyecto Especial Arqueologico Caral-Supe. http://www.caralperu.gob.pe/.

Public Broadcasting Service. "America's Stone Age Explorers." Transcript of broadcast. *Nova,* November 9, 2004. http://www.pbs.org/wgbh/nova/transcripts/3116_stoneage.html.

―――. "Cracking the Maya Code." Transcript of broadcast. *Nova,* April 8, 2008. http://www.pbs.org/wgbh/nova/transcripts/3506_mayacode.html.

―――. "The Mystery of the First Americans." Transcript of broad-cast. *Nova,* December 15, 2000. http://www.pbs.org/wgbh/nova/transcripts/2705first.html.

Roach, John. "Saving the Potato in its Andean Birthplace." *National Geographic,* June 10, 2002. http://news.nationalgeographic.com/ news/2002/06/0610_020610_potato.html.

———. "Superdirt Made Amazon Cities Possible?" *National Geographic,* November 19, 2008. http://news.nationalgeographic.com/ news/2008/11/081119-lost-cities-amazon.html.

Rose, Mark. "The Importance of Monte Verde." *Archaeology,* October 18, 1999. http://www.archaeology.org/online/features/clovis/rose1.html.

Sample, Ian. "Sophisticated Hunters Not to Blame for Driving Mammoths to Extinction." *Guardian* (UK), November 19, 2009. http://www.guardian.co.uk/science/2009/nov/19/hunters-mammoths-extinction.

Schurr, Theodore. "Mitochondrial DNA and the Peopling of the New World." *American Scientist* 88 (May/June 2000). http://www.americanscientist.org/issues/feature/2000/3/mitochondrial-dna-and-the-peopling-of-the-new-world.

Schwartz, John. "The Great Food Migration." *Newsweek* 118 (Special Issue Fall/Winter 1991): 58–62. http://www.millersville.edu/~columbus/data/art/SCHWART1.ART.

Smith, Michael E. "Life in the Provinces of the Aztec Empire." *Scientific American* 15 (Special Issue 2005): 90–97. http://isites.harvard.edu/fs/docs/icb.topic224149.files/Smith_1997.pdf.

Spotts, Peter N. "New Clues to Ancient Mississippi Culture." *Christian Science Monitor,* December 19, 2002. http://www.csmonitor.com/2002/1219/p14s01-stgn.html.

Stevens, William K. "Rediscovering the Lost Crops of the Incas." *New York Times,* October 31, 1989. http://www.nytimes.com/1989/10/31/science/rediscovering-the-lost-crops-of-the-incas.html?pagewanted=1.

Tamm, Erika, Toomas Kivisild, Maere Reidla, Mait Metspalu, David Glenn Smith, Connie J. Mulligan, Claudio M. Bravi, Olga Rickards, Cristina Martinez-Labarga, Elsa K. Khusnutdinova, Sardana A. Fedorova, Maria V. Golubenko, Vadim A. Stepanov, Marina A. Gubina, Sergey I. Zhadanov, Ludmila P. Ossipova, Larisa Damba, Mikhail I. Voevoda, Jose E. Dipierri, Richard Villems, and Ripan S. Malhi. "Beringian Standstill and Spread of Native American Founders." PLoS ONE 2 (2007). http://www.plosone. org/article/info%3Adoi%2F10.1371%2Fjournal.pone.0000829.

Tankersley, Kenneth B. "The Puzzle of the First Americans." *Discovering Archaeology* 2 (January/February 2000). http://www.panhandlenation. com/history/prehistory/disc_arc/intro.htm.

Tennesen, Michael. "Black Gold of the Amazon." *Discover,* April 30, 2007. http://discovermagazine.com/2007/apr/black-gold-of-the-amazon/ article_view?b_start:int=3&-C=.

Tyson, Peter. "End of the Big Beasts." *Nova*, March 1, 2009. http://www. pbs.org/wgbh/nova/stoneage/megafauna.html.

University of Colorado at Boulder. "13,000 Clovis-Era Tool Cache Unearthed in Colorado Shows Evidence of Camel, Horse Butchering." Press release, February 25, 2009. http://www.eurekalert.org/pub_ releases/2009-02/uoca-1ct022509.php.

University of Copenhagen. "The Voyage to America." Press release, April 3, 2008. http://www.eurekalert.org/pub_releases/2008-04/uoc-tvt040308. php.

University of Florida. "'Pristine' Amazonian Region Hosted Large, Urban Civilization, Study Finds." News release, August 28, 2008. http://news. ufl.edu/2008/08/28/urban-amazon/.

———. "Scientists: Earthquakes, El Ninos Fatal to Earliest Civilization in Americas." News release, January 19, 2009. http://www.eurekalert.org/ pub_releases/2009-01/uof-see011509.php.

Wade, Nicholas. "New Data Shed Light on Large-Animal Extinction." *New York Times,* November 19, 2009. http://www.nytimes.com/2009/11/24/science/24fauna.html?_r=1.

Wang, Sijia, Cecil M. Lewis, Jr., Mattias Jakobsson, Sohini Ramachandran, Nicolas Ray, Gabriel Bedoya, Winston Rojas, Maria V. Parra, Julio A. Molina, Carla Gallo, Guido Mazzotti, Giovanni Poletti, Kim Hill, Ana M. Hurtado, Damian Labuda, William Klitz, Ramiro Barrantes, Maria Cátira Bortolini, Francisco M. Salzano, Maria Luiza Petzl-Erler, Luiza T. Tsuneto, Elena Llop, Francisco Rothhammer, Laurent Excoffier, Marcus W. Feldman, Noah A. Rosenberg, and Andrés Ruiz-Linares. "Genetic Variation and Population Structure in Native Americans." *PLoS Genetics* 3 (2007). http://www.plosgenetics.org/article/info:doi/10.1371/journal.pgen.0030185.

Weiner, Debra. "Lunar Eclipse." *Newsweek,* October 16, 2009. http://www.newsweek.com/id/218178.

Wessel, Thomas. "Agriculture, Indians, and American History." *Agricultural History* 50 (January 1976): 9–20. http://www.cals.ncsu.edu/agexed/aee501/indians.html.

Wilford, John Noble. "Chilean Field Yields New Clues to Peopling of Americas." *New York Times,* August 25, 1998. http://www.nytimes.com/1998/08/25/science/chilean-field-yields-new-clues-to-peopling-of-americas.html.

———. "Evidence of Ancient Civilization is Found in Peruvian Countryside." *New York Times,* December 28, 2004. http://query.nytimes.com/gst/fullpage.html?res=950CE2D91F30F93BA15751C1A9629C8B63&sec=&spon=&pagewanted=all.

———. "Symbols on the Wall Push Back Maya Writing by Years." *New York Times,* January 10, 2006. http://www.nytimes.com/2006/01/10/science/10maya.html?_r=1.

Williams, Patrick Ryan, and Donna J. Nash. "Clash of the Andean Titans: Wari and Tiwanaku at Cerro Baúl." *In the Field* (Summer 2003). http://fm1.fieldmuseum.org/aa/Files/rwilliams/WilliamsITF.pdf.

Yukon Beringia Interpretive Center. http://www.beringia.com/.

Zazula, Grant D., Duane G. Froese, Charles E. Schweger, Rolf W. Mathewes, Alwynne B. Beaudoin, Alice M. Telka, C. Richard Harington, and John A. Westgate. "Paleobotany: Ice-Age Steppe Vegetation in East Beringia." *Nature* 423 (June 5, 2003). http://www.nature.com/nature/journal/v423/n6940/abs/423603a.html.

Other media

British Broadcasting Corporation. "The Lost Pyramids of Caral." *Horizon*, January 31, 2002, via Google Video. http://video.google.com/videoplay?docid=-7590203755477313077&hl=es&fs=true#.

National Public Radio. "The Ancient City on the Mississippi." *On Point with Jacki Lyden,* September 3, 2009. http://www.onpointradio.org/2009/09/the-ancient-city-on-the-mississippi.

National Public Radio. "With Climate Swing, a Culture Bloomed in Americas." *All Things Considered,* February 11, 2008. http://www.npr.org/templates/story/story.php?storyId=18888119.

Public Broadcasting Service. "The Fenn Cache" (Clovis-era tools). *Nova,* undated. Photo gallery. http://www.pbs.org/wgbh/nova/stoneage/fenn.html.

———. "Last Extinction." Undated. Video with transcript. http://www.pbs.org/wgbh/nova/clovis/program.html.

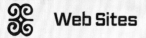 **Web Sites**

Center for the Study of the First Americans at Texas A&M University
http://www.centerfirstamericans.com/

Field Museum: History of Chocolate
http://www.fieldmuseum.org/Chocolate/history_mesoamerican.html

National Climatic Data Center: Atlas of Beringia
http://www.ncdc.noaa.gov/paleo/parcs/atlas/beringia/index.html

National Museum of the American Indian
http://www.nmai.si.edu/

National Oceanic and Atmospheric Administration: Canoes of the Northwest
http://oceanexplorer.noaa.gov/projects/02tribal/canoe_tech/canoe_tech.html

Newberry Library: Ayers Art Collection, American Indian
http://collections.carli.illinois.edu/cdm4/index_nby_ayerart.php?CISOROOT=/nby_ayerart

Textile Museum of Canada
http://www.textilemuseum.ca/cloth_clay/home.html

Welcome to the Mesoamerican Ballgame
http://www.ballgame.org/

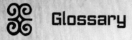 **Glossary**

Beringia: The land mass that linked Asia and North America, stretching from the Lena River in Siberia to the Mackenzie River in North America.

Clovis: A widespread Paleo-Indian culture that produced distinctive spear tips, called Clovis points. The Clovis people fastened these tips to wooden shafts and used the projectile as a hunting weapon. Their namesake is Clovis, New Mexico, where the first Clovis points were identified in 1929.

Columbian Exchange: The unprecedented exchange of plants, animals, human populations, ideas, and diseases between the Western Hemisphere and the Old World.

Mesoamerica: Literally: the middle of the Americas; in archaeology and geography: the area from central Mexico south to parts of Nicaragua. *Meso* is from the Greek word *mesos*, or "middle."

Mexica (MEESH-ih-ka): The dominant culture in Mesoamerica when Europeans arrived in the Western Hemisphere. Often called the Aztec, historians consider that term inaccurate, as none of the peoples of Mesoamerica used it to describe themselves.

milpa: A practice developed by the Maya or adapted by them from a similar system used by other Mesoamericans. Farmers grew several crops grow together in a *milpa* and usually farmed a given piece of land for only a few years before moving on so as not to exhaust the soil.

Paleo-Indians: Inhabitants of the Western Hemisphere prior to 6,000 BC. *Paleo* is from the Greek word *palaios*, or "ancient."

🙰 Index

Picture Credits